Baptism,

Truths Beyond the Waters

Randy Short

2025

Foreword by **Ricardo Sobral**

Title: **BAPTISM: Truths Beyond the Waters**

Author: Randy Short

Proofreader: Kathy Short

Images: Randy Short and Netto Damasceno

All references and quotations of the Bible are taken from the
New King James Version Copyright © 1982 by Thomas Nelson,
Inc. unless otherwise noted.

ISBN 978-65-01-80524-5

© 2025

Table of Contents

DEDICATION

I dedicate this book to the teaching and support staff of the EBNESR Ministry Training School and the EBNESR Publishing House in Recife Brazil for their untiring effort to get the truth of the Bible out both in written and spoken form.

FOREWORD

It is with immense pleasure that I recommend the book, *Baptism: Truths Beyond the Waters*, so beautifully written by my friend, professor, and first and former president of EBNESR Ministry Training School in Recife, Brazil, Randy Short. This book is well worth the investment, not only for its clarification on baptism, but especially for its motivation to commit to Christ and his church through immersion in water.

For my part, I was impressed as I read this work. I could not help but be reminded of Spurgeon, when he presented his exegetical thoughts on **Romans 6:3-4**.

> *"I SHALL not enter into controversy over this text, although over it some have raised the question of infant baptism or believers' baptism, immersion or sprinkling. If any persons can give a consistent and instructive interpretation of the text, otherwise than by assuming believers' immersion to be Christian baptism, I should like to see them do it."*[1]

---

[1]SPURGEON, Charles Haddon, **Baptism:** A Burial. Newington. London: Metropolitan Tabernacle, 1881.

Certainly, Professor Randy Short would also be endorsed, not only by me, but also by the great preacher of his time, Charles Haddon Spurgeon, since the book, *Baptism: Truths Beyond the Waters*, is presented sincerely and coherently, recognizing baptism as a doctrine that must be followed. Professor Randy Short, applying scientific hermeneutical and exegetical tools, combats those who obscure the doctrine of baptism by going beyond what is written in the Word of God.

Baptism: Truths Beyond the Waters offers a frank, sincere, and unprejudiced approach to the subject of baptism. As presented in its introduction, the work becomes an effective tool against any opposing idea, since it bases its statements solely and exclusively on Scripture. This leads its author to carefully explain the doctrine of water baptism for salvation, without fear, trepidation, or apprehension, which unfortunately many pastors and teachers of various denominations fail to do.

Furthermore, Professor Randy Short does not promote his work in a controversial or dogmatic manner, as if he believes he has the last word on the subject. No, the goal of this book, especially chapters three, four, and five, is to lead ordinary people to an understanding of the Scriptures on the subject, and consequently, to protect them from those who teach doctrines that go beyond what the Bible says, as well as from those who lead many into error.

The author concludes his work by presenting baptism as a commitment to the truth presented by Christ for those who desire to be his disciples. Professor Randy Short shows that the disciple's new life, obtained through baptism, is something entirely new since they have been called to walk in newness of life. The work, *"Baptism, Truths Beyond the Waters,"* in its concluding chapter, presents the disciple with a new life, entirely different from the life they had before their baptism. A life as a new creation, believing in Jesus as their Lord and awaiting the glory that will be revealed by virtue of their union with Christ.

That said, I pray that Professor Randy Short's beautifully written book, *"Baptism: Truths Beyond the Waters,"* will be read, studied, and practiced. Baptism is a biblical doctrine that must be followed by all who seek the salvation of their souls by believing that Jesus Christ is Lord.

Ricardo Sobral
President and teacher of the
EBNESR Ministry Training School in Recife, Brazil

Chapter 1
First Things First

Introduction

This book just might challenge your beliefs about baptism like no other book ever has. You will have to decide. Should I continue to believe what I have been taught, or should I change and accept what the Bible teaches?

This book is based exclusively on the Bible. The truth is that not all teachings on baptism in today's religious world can be correct, as the Bible has only one teaching on baptism. Each student of this book must make a prior decision. Do you believe what the Bible says about baptism, or do you think we have the right to change its teachings for today? Do you believe there is a single standard of faith and practice for all disciples today, or do you believe there are multiple truths on this and other subjects?

This book is for you if you believe that the Bible has one standard of faith and behavior for all who call themselves Christians today.

How can we agree on the true teaching regarding baptism?

Will you accept what the Bible teaches about baptism or what your church taught?

I know you believe your church teaches the truth about baptism and they might.

I hope the church you attend teaches exactly what the Bible says. I do not know your church, but in my experience with churches in general, there are many different teachings on baptism, and they are often contradictory.

Interestingly, in all the teachings on baptism in the Bible, you will not find anyone questioning how or why one should be baptized. The apostles, prophets, and evangelists simply asked their listeners to be baptized, and the listener accepted the message and was baptized. They taught this doctrine inspired by God's Holy Spirit, and there was no room for doubt.

Today, with so many churches teaching different things, there is confusion on the subject. This confusion leads people to question baptism:

How should baptism be done?
> Sprinkle with water?
> Pouring water?
> Immersion in water?

Why should someone be baptized? Does a person have to be baptized to be saved? If a person is to be baptized, who can baptize them? Who can be baptized and who should not be baptized? If a person did not understand what the Bible says about baptism before being baptized, was their baptism valid? Many more questions are raised about baptism today but if you study through the New Testament you will not find these, or any other questions mentioned.

Sometimes, to see and understand the truth about a subject, we must first deconstruct what has been erroneously taught.

Again, the basis of our study is not any church's creed, but rather the Word of God. We have a closed biblical canon for almost 2,000 years.[2] We do not need anything else.

Paul wrote the following to Timothy:
> *All Scripture is given by inspiration of God, and is profitable for doctrine, for reproof, for correction, for instruction in righteousness, that the man of*

---

[2] The biblical canon or canon of Scripture is the list of religious texts (or "books") that a given community accepts as being inspired by God and authoritative. The word "canon" comes from the Greek term κανών ("ruler" or "measuring stick"). https://pt.wikipedia.org/wiki/Cânon_bíblico

God may be complete, thoroughly equipped for every good work. **2 Timothy 3:16-17**

This means that in the God-breathed Scriptures we have everything we need to be perfect and thoroughly equipped for every good work. We need nothing more, or else Paul was wrong.

Pedro said the following to his readers and to us:
> as *His divine power has given to us all things that pertain to life and godliness, through the knowledge of Him who called us by glory and virtue, by which have been given to us exceedingly great and precious promises, that through these you may be partakers of the divine nature, having escaped the corruption that is in the world through lust.* **2 Peter 1:3-4**

Do we need anything more to have life and godliness? Peter said 2,000 years ago that we have already received complete knowledge, "all things".

Do you believe Peter, or do you still need more revelations?

Jude told the people who received his letter things that we also need to know:

Beloved, while I was very diligent to write to you concerning our common salvation, I found it necessary to write to you exhorting you to contend earnestly for the faith which was once for all delivered to the saints. **Jude 1:3**

"The faith" (concerning our common salvation) was delivered to the saints once for all 2,000 years ago, and all that remains for us is to defend those truths. We do not have to look for modern revelations. We must defend what we have had for 2,000 years.

We Don't Need Anything Else!

According to these texts we do not need anything else!

2 Timothy 3:16-17 – The Scriptures that we have are able to make a man perfect, thoroughly furnished for every good work. Do you believe it?

Jude 1:3 – Jude said that it only remains to diligently defend the faith because it was once for all delivered to the saints. Do you believe it?

2 Peter 1:3-4 – 2,000 years ago Peter said that God has already given all things that pertain to life and godliness.

Do you believe it?

First Things First		
WE DON'T NEED ANYTHING ELSE **2 Timothy 3:16-17** All Scripture *is* given by inspiration of God, and *is* profitable for doctrine, for reproof, for correction, for instruction in righteousness, that the man of God may be complete, thoroughly equipped for every good work. **Do you believe it?**	**WE DON'T NEED ANYTHING ELSE** **Judas 1:3** Beloved, while I was very diligent to write to you concerning our common salvation, I found it necessary to write to you exhorting you to contend earnestly for the faith which was <u>once for all</u> delivered to the saints. **Do you believe it?**	**WE DON'T NEED ANYTHING ELSE** **2 Pedro 1:3-4** **2,000 years ago Peter said, ...** His divine power has given to us <u>all things</u> that *pertain* to life and godliness, through the knowledge of Him who called us by glory and virtue, by which have been given to us **Do you believe it?**

If you truly believe these verses, you will not seek modern revelations and you will follow and defend God's Word as it is written.

If you genuinely believe these verses you will not seek modern revelations and you will follow and defend the Word of God as it is written.

Has anything changed in these years? Can we change God's law? Well, church teachings change— but we must never change God's teaching, and it has always been that way.

Moses, about 3,500 years ago, said to the people of Israel:

> *Now, O Israel, listen to the statutes and the judgments which I teach you to observe, that you may live, and go in and possess the land which the*

11

LORD God of your fathers is giving you. You shall not add to the word which I command you, nor take from it, that you may keep the commandments of the LORD your God which I command you. **Deuteronomy 4:1-2**

He spoke about the law and covenant of God's People at that time, but this establishes a rule for all time.

The wise man wrote.
Every word of God is pure; He is a shield to those who put their trust in Him. Do not add to His words, Lest He rebuke you, and you be found a liar. **Proverbs 30:5-6**

When someone adds to God's Word, they are adding human ideas and directing their own steps. Look at what the prophet Jeremiah said wisely about this.
O LORD, I know the way of man is not in himself; It is not in man who walks to direct his own steps. **Jeremiah 10:23**

It is not up to man to decide these things. God has already spoken what he wants.

Jeremiah also further explained why this is true:

> *The heart is deceitful above all things, and desperately wicked; who can know it?* **Jeremiah 17:9**

Another wise man also explained:

> *There is a way that seems right to a man, but its end is the way of death.* **Proverbs 14:12**

We cannot trust our own steps and hearts. Only God, who created us, is wise enough to determine our steps.

Someone might say, "But wait a minute! This is all from the Old Testament and the Old Covenant. We have a New Covenant to follow." That is true, but the principle that we must respect what God has spoken and not alter it has been established for all of God's law in every age.

If you are looking for a teaching that comes directly from the New Covenant of Christ Jesus, then here we go: the New Testament also says that man should not add anything to it. For example, Paul writes:

> *Now these things, brethren, I have figuratively transferred to myself and Apollos for your sakes, that you may learn in us not to think beyond what*

is written, that none of you may be puffed up on behalf of one against the other. **1 Corinthians 4:6**

Do not go beyond what is written, Paul said.

What the apostle John said in Revelation sounds remarkably like something Moses said in **Deuteronomy 4:1-2**. John wrote:

For I testify to everyone who hears the words of the prophecy of this book: If anyone adds to these things, God will add to him the plagues that are written in this book; and if anyone takes away from the words of the book of this prophecy, God shall take away his part from the Book of Life, from the holy city, and from the things which are written in this book. **Revelation 22:18-19**

From the beginning of the Bible, some 3,500 years ago, through the entire Old Testament, to the end of the New Testament, and finally to the end of the Bible, what do we find? Add nothing to, and take nothing away from, God's Word. What the Bible teaches about baptism should be our belief, practice, and teaching to others, without adding or taking anything away.

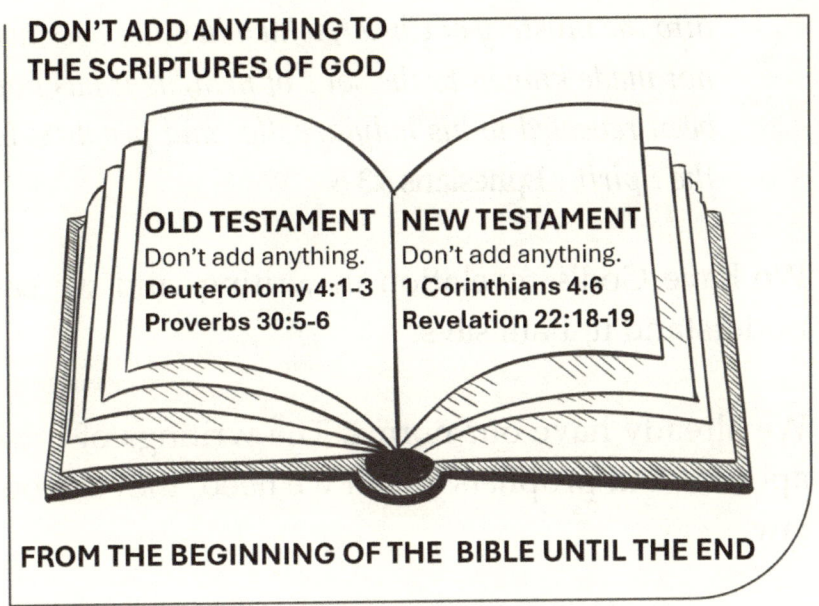

DON'T ADD ANYTHING TO THE SCRIPTURES OF GOD

OLD TESTAMENT	NEW TESTAMENT
Don't add anything.	Don't add anything.
Deuteronomy 4:1-3	**1 Corinthians 4:6**
Proverbs 30:5-6	**Revelation 22:18-19**

FROM THE BEGINNING OF THE BIBLE UNTIL THE END

Obviously, this does not just apply to baptism. We should not add anything to anything God has already spoken about.

Sometimes people say that "God revealed this or that to me." That is dangerous talk!

God revealed his will to the apostles and prophets 2,000 years ago, they recorded it and it is up to us to read, believe, practice, and teach it.

Paul says the following in his letter.

For by revelation it was made known to me the mystery, as I wrote a little while ago briefly, so that when you read, you may understand my insight

15

into the mystery of Christ, which in other ages was not made known to the sons of men, as it has now been revealed to his holy apostles and prophets by the Spirit . **Ephesians 3:3-5**

We have God's revelation in writing, and we can understand it, Paul says.

We already have our norms. The writings of these apostles and prophets are all we need; they are our law.

Paul said:

> *To those who are without law, as without law (not being without law toward God, but under law toward Christ), that I might win those who are without law.* **1 Corinthians 9:21**

In this context, he is talking about rights he had and gave up to win as many people as possible to Christ. He also identifies something he would never give up: the law of Christ. "Under the law of Christ," Paul says. Yes, we have the law of Christ, and we must be obedient to it and never think of going beyond it, taking from it, or adding to it.

James calls this law the perfect law.

But he who looks into the perfect law of liberty and continues in it and is not a forgetful hearer but a doer of the work, this one will be blessed in what he does. **James 1:25**

The perfect law does not need man's help. There is no need for new revelations. This is the law of liberty, through which we can be set free. **John 8:32**

Look at the context in which James wrote what he said in verse **25**.

But be doers of the word, and not hearers only, deceiving yourselves. For if anyone is a hearer of the word and not a doer, he is like a man observing his natural face in a mirror; for he observes himself, goes away, and immediately forgets what kind of man he was. **James 1:22-24**

We have a law. We must neither add to nor subtract from it. Why? Because it is perfect. James concludes: There is no point in knowing these truths if we do not become "doers" of them.

Then he further exhorts.

So speak and so do as those who will be judged by the law of liberty. **James 2:12**

We must obey this law of liberty because we will be judged according to our conduct in accordance with or divergence with the law. What this law says about baptism is what we must believe, practice, and teach. This is what we will see in these studies.

Let us be careful not to fall into the sin of presumption.[3] Assuming we know what pleases God without God having spoken is beyond dangerous!

Presumption is a sin, a great transgression! The psalmist David said:

> Keep back Your servant also from presumptuous sins; Let them not have dominion over me. Then I shall be blameless, And I shall be innocent of great transgression. **Psalm 19:13**

Presumption is a sin when it comes to the things of God. Can we say, "Oh, God doesn't care about that. Baptism can be done by immersion, sprinkling, or pouring water on the head"?

---

[3] Conjecture: act of presuming; judgment not based on evidence, appearances; supposition that is taken as true, but without proof.

THE MIND OF GOD
No one understands
Isaiah 55:8-9

God recorded His
will in the Bible.
Psalm 119:130. 2 Timothy 3:16-17
The mind of man cannot
understand beyond
what God has revealed.
1 Corinthians 2:4-5, 10, 2 Peter 1:20-21
If a man says he knows the will of God
beyond what is revealed that is the sin
presumption.
Psalm 19:13

THE SIN OF PRESUMPTION
If God has not revealed
His will on a subject, then
to claim that you know
what God wants is the sin
of presumption.

Unfortunately, there are those who act, teach and proceed as if the things they believe came from the Lord.

How can we say, "I know God approves this," when He has not revealed Himself in this regard?

Our thoughts are inferior to God's. God himself said through his prophet Isaiah:

For My thoughts are not your thoughts, nor are your ways My ways," says the LORD. "For as the heavens are higher than the earth, so are My ways higher than your ways, And My thoughts than your thoughts. **Isaiah 55:8-9**

We can know God's will only through God's written revelation. Anything beyond this is speculation and sin.

19

Surprisingly, people often assume they can act, teach, and proceed differently from what the Lord wrote, and yet still dare to call it God's will. To justify human action, to soothe their own conscience and silence the inner call to submit to God's Word, we often hear phrases like these:

- "God is our Heavenly Father. He loves us! Doesn't He want us to be happy? I know my Father wants me to do this because it will make me happy!"

- "God may have been strict in the Old Testament, but in the New Testament we are under a system of grace. Therefore, we are not in bondage to worry about keeping all the laws perfectly. We don't need to worry about these tedious and detailed observations."

- "Do you really think God would send me to Hell just for doing this or teaching it? Would God really condemn me for this one sin? My God is not like that!"

- "What is so bad about doing this? No one will be harmed if we do it this way."

These common questions embody the very spirit of presumption because they set aside what God has said in favor of human rationalization. A true servant of God will stick as closely as possible to what God inspired men to write in the Bible. The further one strays from the clear words of Scripture, the more the intentions of one's own heart are revealed.

Conclusion

What does God think about baptism? What does the Bible say? We will not seek what men think about baptism today. We will search within the sacred pages for what men, inspired by the Holy Spirit, believed, practiced, and taught about baptism.

If you do not agree that we should only believe, obey and teach what the Bible says then the arguments presented in this book will be of little influence on you. If you do agree that the Bible is our only guide to our faith and practice today you might need to make some difficult changes about what you believe and have practiced concerning baptism.

CHAPTER 2
What Does the Word "Baptism" Mean?

The Original Meaning of the Word

There are many words found in different Bible translations that are not translated; they are transliterations.[4] Consider some key words in the New Testament. Words like "presbyter," "Christ," "baptism," "angel," and "apostle" are not translations from Greek into English. They are rather transliterations. The Greek letters of a word are brought over to the corresponding letter in the English alphabet or similar sounding letters. This happens in other language translations as well.

When scholars began translating the Old and New Testaments into English and other languages, they faced enormous challenges.

At times powerful figures objected to translating certain words of Scripture with their true meaning and so opted for transliteration thus hiding the true meaning. They did this because the true translation would not match the current practice in their churches.

---

[4] Transliteration is the process of transferring a word from one language's alphabet to another. Transliteration helps people pronounce words and names in foreign languages by exchanging the letters of the word's original alphabet for similar-sounding letters in a different language. – Webster's Dictionary

The book, *A History of the Baptism Apostasy* by Cecil N. Wright documents the historical evolution of baptismal practices within Christianity. It notes that the 1311 Council of Ravenna officially permitted sprinkling as a choice for baptism, not just an exception for emergencies. Translations after this chose to transliterate the Greek word.

Some Biblical scholars suggest that King James and his translators deliberately transliterated the word to avoid controversy, as pouring and sprinkling were the established religious practices at the time.

It might also be that the languages themselves lacked all the words necessary to meaningfully reproduce what the original languages were saying and so the option was transliteration. That is not true of this word.

Even if you do not know Greek the following chart will help you understand how our word baptism came about.

$A\alpha$ Alpha	$B\beta$ Beta	$\Gamma\gamma$ Gamma	$\Delta\delta$ Delta	$E\varepsilon$ Epsilon	$Z\zeta$ Zeta
$H\eta$ Eta	$\Theta\theta$ Theta	$I\iota$ Iota	$K\kappa$ Kappa	$\Lambda\lambda$ Lambda	$M\mu$ Mu
$N\nu$ Nu	$\Xi\xi$ Ksi	Oo Omicron	$\Pi\pi$ Pi	$P\rho$ Rho	$\Sigma\sigma$ Sigma
$T\tau$ Tau	$Y\upsilon$ Upsilon	$\Phi\varphi$ Phi	$X\chi$ Chi	$\Psi\psi$ Psi	$\Omega\omega$ Omega

Exercise

$$\beta\ \acute{\alpha}\ \pi\ \tau\ \iota\ \sigma\ \mu\ \alpha$$

$$\downarrow\ \downarrow\ \ \downarrow\ \downarrow\ \downarrow\ \downarrow\ \downarrow\ \ \downarrow$$

$$b\ a\ p\ t\ i\ s\ m\ a$$

Transliteration

The words "baptism" (Greek: βάπτισμα) and "baptize" (Greek: βαπτίζω) were not translated. Why? In this case history tells us that ecclesiastical[5] authorities felt that expressing the true meaning of this word would cause controversy within the churches. The usage at that time did not agree with the original meaning of the Greek word. This means

[5] Side note: Ecclesiastical is also a transliterated word and comes from the Greek word for "church" or "assembly".

that the original meaning was, over the centuries, conveniently hidden and replaced by practices that differed from the true meaning of the Greek word.

Let us take a modern dictionary and look up the meaning of the word "baptism":

> *"Baptism is a rite, normally performed with water on the initiate, through immersion, effusion or sprinkling."*[6]

But we have a problem here: this is the modern meaning—or at least it includes the modern meanings. What we want to know is what Jesus Christ meant when this word came from his mouth. We want to know when inspired men like Paul and Peter spoke or wrote this word, what they understood it to mean. We should not concern ourselves with modern dictionaries or the religious ones of our time.

What is the Biblical meaning of this word?

The word in the first century meant "immersion in water."[7] The Greek verb βαπτίζω, *baptizo* (found 77 times in the Bible) means "to plunge into or under,"

---

6 Wikipedia. https://pt.wikipedia.org/wiki/Batismo
7 From the dictionary of Henry George Liddell and Robert Scott.

"to sink," "to plunge[8]." These meanings come from two of the most respected dictionaries of Biblical Greek.[9]

If Jesus or one of the apostles meant to say, "pour water on a person's head," there was a Greek word for it, εκχύνω (*ekchyno*). Peter used this word.

> *And it shall come to pass in the last days, saith the Lord, that I will __pour__ out of my Spirit upon all flesh...* **Acts 2:17**

In Hebrews, the author spoke of what happened when the High Priest entered the Holy of Holies once a year; he sprinkled animal blood inside. The Greek word is ραντίζω (*rantizo*).

> *Wherefore if the blood of goats and of bulls, and the ashes of a heifer, __sprinkled__ upon them that are defiled, sanctify them to the purifying of the flesh.* **Hebrews 9:13**

If Jesus wanted to authorize sprinkling he would have used this word, but he never used it to identify the mode of baptism.

---

[8] Kittel 1985.
[9] Liddell–Scott–Jones (LSJ), Kittel

Graphic

The Greek word rantizo means sprinkle and never means baptism.

The Greek word ekcheo means pour and never means baptism.

The Greek word baptizo means immersion and never means pouring or sprinkling.

The Greek words with these distinct meanings can be clearly seen in the translation of the Old Testament, in the Greek version called *the Septuagint.*[10]

> *And the priest shall take some of the log of oil and pour it into the palm of his own left hand. Then the priest shall dip his right finger in the oil that is in his left hand and shall sprinkle some of the oil with his finger seven times before the LORD.* **Leviticus 14:15-16**

---

[10] *Septuagint* is the name of the version of the **Hebrew Bible** translated in stages into **Koine Greek (of the New Testament era)**, between the 3rd century BC and the 1st century BC, in **Alexandria**.
https://pt.wikipedia.org/wiki/Septuaginta

Jesus never commanded people to be sprinkled or water to be poured on their heads, nor did the apostles and prophets, inspired by the Holy Spirit, say that immersion could be replaced by these ideas. They always used the verb βαπτίζω, meaning "to immerse." We should say and do the same.

You might be thinking, "Wow! So, I will have to learn Greek to understand the Bible?" No, it is not necessary. We can clearly see from biblical examples that baptism in the Bible was always by immersion.

Biblical Examples
John the Baptist practiced baptism by immersion.

Mark recorded the following about John's baptism.
> Then all the land of Judea, and those from Jerusalem, went out to him and were all baptized by him in the Jordan River, confessing their sins. **Mark 1:5**

Sprinkled in the Jordan River? Having water poured on their heads in the Jordan River? It only makes sense to say that they were immersed by him in the Jordan River.

30

Still about John the Baptist, the apostle John writes:

> Now John also was baptizing in Aenon near Salim because there was much water there. And they came and were baptized. **John 3:23**

How was Jesus baptized?

Jesus came and was baptized by John in the Jordan river.
Then the Bible says "coming up from the water."

- Jesus went into the water.
- John immersed Him in the water.
- Afterwards Jesus came out of the water.

Mark 1:9-10

It is possible to immerse people in rivers. To sprinkle, you do not even need to go to a river. But to immerse someone, you need a lot of water. To sprinkle, just a little bit is enough. John the Baptist chose a place where there was plenty of water.

Jesus was baptized by immersion.

Mark also records:

> *It came to pass in those days that Jesus came from Nazareth of Galilee and was baptized by John in the Jordan. And immediately, coming up from the*

water, He saw the heavens parting and the Spirit descending upon Him like a dove. in **Mark 1:9-10**

Jesus entered the water. He was baptized in the Jordan River. Then he came up out of the water. In this example, could we say that Jesus' baptism was by sprinkling or by pouring water? Obviously not.

Philip and the eunuch

The evangelists also continued this practice of immersion after Jesus returned to heaven. There is no reason to believe that in the first century, baptism was anything other than immersion in water.

Luke speaks extensively about baptism in the book of Acts. A passage that also clearly demonstrates, by example, that baptism was by immersion is found in **Acts 8:26-40**: Here we have the story of Philip the evangelist and the eunuch from Ethiopia, whom he, Philip, was called to evangelize. The eunuch was reading a prophecy about Jesus in the book of Isaiah, but he did not understand what he was reading. Philip approached the chariot and asked him, *"Do you understand what you are reading?"* and the eunuch asked for help. Philip, beginning with that same passage of scripture, *"preached Jesus to him,"* Luke reports.

The summary of Philip's message to the eunuch was simply Jesus. But certainly, included in that message was faith in Jesus, repentance from sins, and baptism, among other things. The eunuch asked, *"Here is water; what prevents me from being baptized?"* Philip replied, *"Nothing, if you believe."* The eunuch answered affirmatively. Look at these verses.

> *So, he commanded the chariot to stand still. And both Philip and the eunuch went down into the water, and he baptized him. Now when they came up out of the water, the Spirit of the Lord caught Philip away...***38-39a**

See, the two got out of the chariot. The two went into the water. Philip baptized the eunuch. The two came out of the water.

Does it make sense to think that this baptism could have been by sprinkling or pouring water? Of course not.

Does it make sense to think this baptism was by sprinkling or pouring water? Of course not.

From these verses, we can clearly see that the biblical form of baptism was immersion, and that the Bible ignores the practice of sprinkling or pouring water. Therefore, the sprinkling practice of the Catholic Church and some denominations is not in accordance with biblical teaching. Even though these practices are called "baptism" by religious authorities, they are not in accordance with the words used by Jesus and the apostles and prophets in the first century. Let the Bible speak and be our guide for our practice today: we will baptize only by immersion.

The Symbolism of Baptism – and the Meaning of the Word

Finally, baptism is a symbol. It is a symbol of Jesus' death, burial, and resurrection. Saying that baptism is a symbol should not reduce it to just a symbol, but we will talk more about this when we discuss the purpose of baptism in another chapter. For now, let us focus on what it symbolizes.

Let us look at the symbolism in **Romans 6:3-4**:

> *Or do you not know that all of us who were baptized into Christ Jesus were baptized into his death? We were therefore buried with him through baptism into death, in order that, just as Christ*

34

was raised from the dead through the glory of the Father, we too might walk in newness of life.

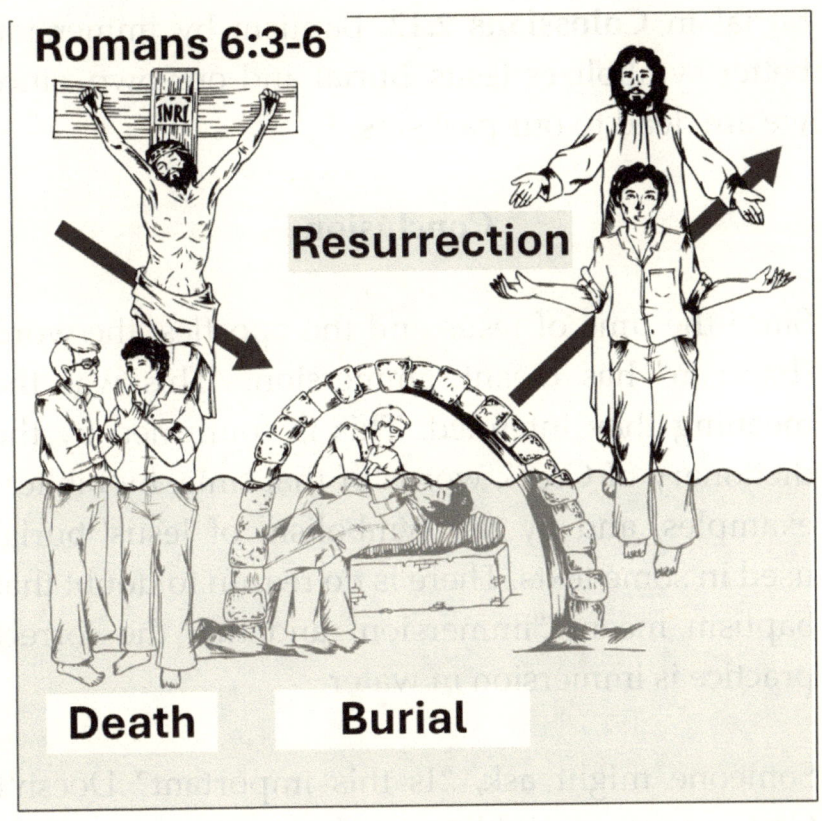

Romans 6:3-6

Resurrection

Death   **Burial**

Just as in the Lord's Supper we take the bread that symbolizes his body and the juice of the vine that symbolizes the blood of Jesus, baptism symbolizes the death, burial, and resurrection of Jesus.

The symbolism is easy to see. Sprinkling or pouring water does not resemble burial. Burial is done by placing the body completely underground (immersion), not just sprinkling a handful of earth over it. Paul also refers to baptism as a symbol of burial in **Colossians 2:12**. Baptism by immersion better symbolizes Jesus' burial and our own, since we are dead to our past sins.

Conclusion

Since the time of Jesus and the apostles, the word "baptism" has meant "immersion." This was the meaning they intended. This is confirmed by the dictionary of Greek words of that time, by biblical examples, and by the symbolism of Jesus' burial used in some texts. There is no reason to doubt that baptism means "immersion" and that the correct practice is immersion in water.

Someone might ask, "Is this important? Doesn't God accept sprinkling and pouring water as baptism?"

Let me answer with a few questions. Can we change the meaning of this word? If we can change the meaning of this word, can we also change the meaning of the word "bread" in the Lord's Supper? Can we change the meaning of the word "repentance"? If we can ignore the change in the meaning of the word "baptism" from that time, what prevents us from changing the meaning of other words and altering the practice and teaching of other biblical doctrines?

As stated in the first chapter, we cannot commit the sin of presumption, presuming to know that God accepts sprinkling and pouring of water when He has not said that. Baptism by immersion is what is clearly spoken of and accepted in the New Testament. Let us practice what we are certain of and leave speculation to others.

CHAPTER 3
What is the Purpose of Baptism? (1)

What Others Say?

Once again, we find a divergence between biblical teaching compared to that of the Catholic Church and that of most evangelical churches. Which of these teachings is biblical? Is there another purpose for baptism in the Bible? Let us see what religions say about the purpose of baptism. Why should someone be baptized? Is baptism truly a necessity?

Look at this series of questions and answer them before reading the answers.

> Who says that whoever is baptized will be saved and then, when an adult, will believe in Jesus?

> If you answered Catholics, you are right. Catholics practice infant baptism, teaching that infants are born with sin and need to be baptized immediately to be cleansed of their sins.

> Who says that "Whoever believes in Jesus will be saved, and that after being discipled for three to six months (or more) they can be baptized to symbolize the salvation they already have?"

If you answered most evangelicals, you are right. According to them, salvation comes when a person hears the call to accept Jesus, they raise their hand to express acceptance and say a prayer inviting Jesus into their heart. Baptism is outside the context of salvation in these churches.

Finally, who said: "Whoever believes and is baptized will be saved?"

If you answered Jesus, you are right. In **Mark 16:16,** Jesus said exactly this::
He who believes and is baptized will be saved," and Jesus ends by saying, *"He who does not believe will be condemned."*

The purpose of *BAPTISM* (part 1)
What do others say.

Who says?

HE WHO IS BAPTIZED ➡️ WILL BE SAVED
AND WILL BELIEVE ONE DAY.

Who says this? Catholics

HE WHO BELIEVES ➡️ WILL BE SAVED
AND ONE DAY WILL BE BAPTIZED.

Who says this? Most evangelicals

HE WHO BELIEVES AND IS BAPTIZED ➡️ WILL BE SAVED

Who said this? Jesus Christ (Mark 16:16)

Which of these three contradictory views of baptism do you accept? I do not know about you, but I stand with Jesus' words.

Jesus spoke these words on the day he ascended into heaven. He gave orders to his disciples (**Acts 1:2, Mark 16:19**). He told them to return to Jerusalem and wait for the promise of the Father, the baptism with the Holy Spirit, and that they should continue preaching the gospel in Jerusalem, Judea, and the Samaria, to the ends of the earth (**Acts 1:8**). Then he was taken up on high.

What the Bible Teaches About the Purpose of Baptism

Was Jesus' teaching on baptism followed by the apostles after his return to heaven and the baptism with the Holy Spirit? Do other biblical passages coincide with Jesus' words in **Mark 16:16**?

On the day of Pentecost, after the baptism with the Holy Spirit, Jesus' apostles preached. Peter's preaching has been preserved for us in **Acts 2**.

When the sermon ended, what was the result?

> *Now when they heard these things, they were cut to the heart, and said to Peter and the rest of the apostles, 'Brothers, what shall we do?' Peter said to them, 'Repent, and let every one of you be baptized in the name of Jesus Christ for the forgiveness of sins, and you will receive the gift of the Holy Spirit.'* **Acts 2:37-38**

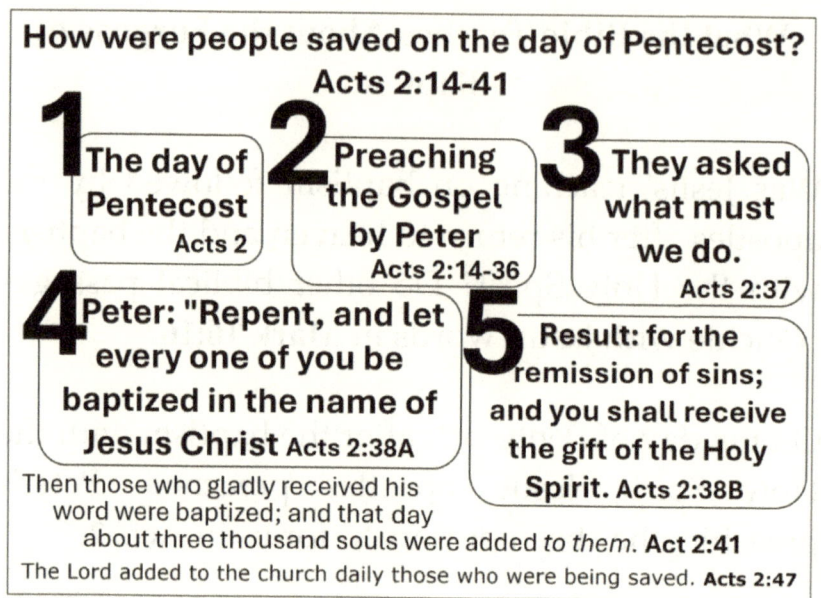

How were people saved on the day of Pentecost?
Acts 2:14-41

1 The day of Pentecost Acts 2

2 Preaching the Gospel by Peter Acts 2:14-36

3 They asked what must we do. Acts 2:37

4 Peter: "Repent, and let every one of you be baptized in the name of Jesus Christ Acts 2:38A

5 Result: for the remission of sins; and you shall receive the gift of the Holy Spirit. Acts 2:38B

Then those who gladly received his word were baptized; and that day about three thousand souls were added to them. Act 2:41

The Lord added to the church daily those who were being saved. Acts 2:47

Peter's words perfectly coincide with Jesus' words. Repent and be baptized, and you will receive two things: the remission (forgiveness) of sins and the gift of the Holy Spirit.

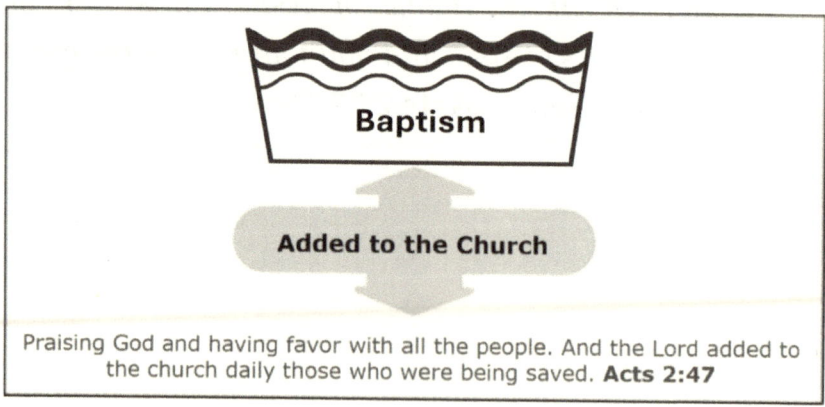

Baptism

Added to the Church

Praising God and having favor with all the people. And the Lord added to the church daily those who were being saved. Acts 2:47

How does the Bible describe salvation? The blessing of eternal salvation is not always described with the same words. Sometimes we will read phrases like "sins washed away," "redeemed from sins," "forgiven of sins," or "saved from sins," and at other times "regenerated" or "remission of sins." All these terms and others indicate the same thing: eternal salvation.

In the example of Saul, the persecutor of the church who was converted and transformed into the great apostle Paul, we can see the importance and purpose of baptism. He himself tells the story of his conversion in **Acts 22,** and in verse **16** he says that Ananias, the Christian God had sent to speak to him, said to him:

> *And now why do you delay? Get up, be baptized, and wash away your sins, calling on his name.*

Here salvation is spoken of as **"washing away sins."** What happens in baptism? Sins are washed away.

When was Paul saved? Many say it was on the road to Damascus. Have you ever heard this phrase? Have you ever repeated it? "Paul was saved on the road to Damascus!" Let us see if it is true.

The story begins in **Acts 9:1**. We learn that Saul, the great persecutor of the church (after his conversion, he is known better as Paul), was going to Damascus with letters giving him permission to enter local synagogues and, if he found Christians there, to arrest them and carry them back to Jerusalem.

> *As he journeyed he came near Damascus, and suddenly a light shone around him from heaven. Then he fell to the ground, and heard a voice saying to him, "Saul, Saul, why are you persecuting Me?" And he said, "Who are You, Lord?" Then the Lord said, "I am Jesus, whom you are persecuting. It is hard for you to kick against the goads." So he, trembling and astonished, said, "Lord, what do You want me to do?" Then the Lord said to him, "Arise and go into the city, and you will be told what you must do.* **Acts 9:3-6**

Jesus did not tell Saul what to do except that he was to go into the city of Damascus and there someone would tell him what to do.

> *And the men who journeyed with him stood speechless, hearing a voice but seeing no one. Then Saul arose from the ground, and when his eyes were opened he saw no one. But they led him by the hand and brought him into Damascus. And he*

was three days without sight, and neither ate nor drank. **Acts 9:7-9**

Saul was struck blind. His companions led him by the hand to Damascus. I am sure that Saul's encounter with Jesus caused him to repent of his sins, especially the way he had treated Christians. Though the Bible does not say it is likely he spent these three days in prayer.

God called on a Christian named Ananias to go and teach Paul what he needed to do. Ananias was not too keen on going to Saul because he had heard of Saul's reputation as a persecutor of Christians. God however explained the importance that Saul would have to the mission and so he went.

And Ananias went his way and entered the house; and laying his hands on him he said, "Brother Saul, the Lord Jesus, who appeared to you on the road as you came, has sent me that you may receive your sight and be filled with the Holy Spirit. **Acts 9:17**

Saul then was cured of his blindness. It might be interesting to note that even though he was cured he still was not saved.

Immediately there fell from his eyes something like scales, and he received his sight at once; and he arose and was baptized. **Acts 9:18**

He did not delay any longer. It had been three days since he had met Jesus, and he realized he was on the wrong path.

Saul later is called Paul. In chapter 22 he recounts what happened to him. He explained that Ananias said,

> *And now why are you waiting? Arise and be baptized, and wash away your sins, calling on the name of the Lord.* **Acts 22:16**

Baptism was the moment Paul's sins were washed away and he was saved, not what happened on the road to Damascus.

Was Paul saved when he began his journey to Damascus? Some people would say yes. Why?

Have you ever heard people say that "all roads lead to Heaven"? "You just need to do what you think is right and you will be saved. A clean heart and a pure conscience are all you need," they say. Well, Paul, at the beginning of his defense before the Sanhedrin, said this:

And Paul, steadfastly looking upon the council, said, Men and brethren, I have lived in all good conscience before God until this day. **Acts 23:1**

When he was Saul, the great persecutor of the church, he did everything in good conscience. Later after defending himself before Governor Felix, he said:

Therefore, I strive to always have a clear conscience before God and men. **Acts 24:16**

Finally, defending himself before King Agrippa Paul said:

Indeed, it seemed to me that I ought to do many things contrary to the name of Jesus of Nazareth. **Acts 26:9**

Paul lived his entire life doing what he thought was right without violating his conscience. But a pure conscience could not save him. He needed to believe in Jesus, surrender his life to Him, and be baptized to have his sins washed away. So, even if someone says Paul was already saved at the beginning of his journey, that is not true.

How was Paul saved?

Were Paul's sins washed away when he met Jesus?

Were Paul's sins washed away when he fasted 3 days?

Were Paul's sins washed away when he was cured?

Were Paul's sins washed away when Ananias preached?

Baptism

Were Paul's sins washed away when he was baptized? YES!

Acts 22:16 And now why are you waiting? Arise and be baptized, and wash away your sins, calling on the name of the Lord.'

One might say, then, that when he met Jesus he was saved, and therefore he would have been saved on the road to Damascus. This sounds true, for even Jesus himself said:

> *And this is eternal life, that they may know you, the only true God, and Jesus Christ, whom you have sent.* **John 17:3**

Knowing God can certainly be considered as eternal life.

Paul also speaks about when Jesus returns from heaven with his mighty angels.

> *in flaming fire taking vengeance on those who do not know God and on those who do not obey the gospel of our Lord Jesus.* **2 Thessalonians 1:8**

Did you understand what Paul said? Jesus will punish those who do not know God *and* those who do not obey the gospel. Paul knew the truth that Jesus was alive on the road to Damascus; but Paul had not yet obeyed the gospel to have his sins washed away. Paul was not saved on the road to Damascus.

There must also be those who say that Paul was saved when Ananias laid his hands on him and he regained his sight—that is, when he was cured of blindness. Physical healing and salvation are not the same thing. Paul, three days after being healed, was still not saved. Nothing in the text indicates this.

After meeting Jesus on the road, Paul spent three more days fasting and probably praying and repenting of his sins.

Some might suggest that the moment he repented of his sins, he was saved. Repentance of sins is certainly necessary for salvation, and I also believe that one of the results of Paul's encounter with Jesus was that he repented of his sins. Jesus preached repentance (**Matthew 4:17**) early in his ministry. In the mission he gave to his disciples before returning to heaven he said:

> *and that repentance and forgiveness of sins should be preached in his name to all nations, beginning from Jerusalem.* **Luke 24:47**

Paul certainly needed to repent of his sins, but the Bible is clear that his sins were washed away when he was baptized. Read again:

> *And now why do you delay? Get up and be baptized and wash away your sins, calling on his name.* **Acts 22:16**

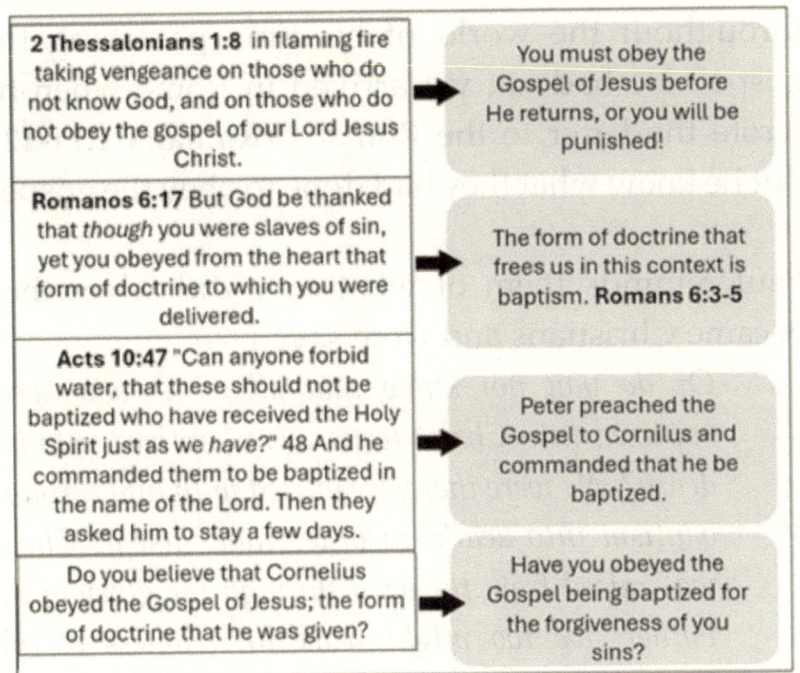

2 Thessalonians 1:8 in flaming fire taking vengeance on those who do not know God, and on those who do not obey the gospel of our Lord Jesus Christ.	You must obey the Gospel of Jesus before He returns, or you will be punished!
Romanos 6:17 But God be thanked that *though* you were slaves of sin, yet you obeyed from the heart that form of doctrine to which you were delivered.	The form of doctrine that frees us in this context is baptism. **Romans 6:3-5**
Acts 10:47 "Can anyone forbid water, that these should not be baptized who have received the Holy Spirit just as we *have?*" 48 And he commanded them to be baptized in the name of the Lord. Then they asked him to stay a few days.	Peter preached the Gospel to Cornilus and commanded that he be baptized.
Do you believe that Cornelius obeyed the Gospel of Jesus; the form of doctrine that he was given?	Have you obeyed the Gospel being baptized for the forgiveness of you sins?

Have you applied these truths to your own life? You have a good conscience. You know Jesus. You have repented of your sins and already surrendered your life to Him, wanting to be saved, but you have not yet been baptized. If this describes your journey, perhaps you feel saved. But aren't you in the same condition as Paul before he was baptized, still with your sins?

How Can We Obey the Gospel?

Saul, after being baptized to wash away his sins, became the great apostle Paul and traveled throughout the world of his time preaching the gospel. He had not yet arrived in Rome when he wrote the letter to the Romans (**Romans 1:11-12**). But he knew what they had done to obey the gospel.

Paul reminds them of what they did when they became Christians and were saved.

> *Or do you not know that all of us who were baptized into Christ Jesus were baptized into his death? We were therefore buried with him through baptism into death, in order that, just as Christ was raised from the dead through the glory of the Father, we too might walk in newness of life.* **Romans 6:3-4**

How did he know if he had never been there? The answer is that everyone, everywhere, who taught the gospel of Jesus said the same thing and did the same thing.

Baptism is the Bible's way of teaching us to obey the gospel. Consider verse **17** in this context. This verse is often not even associated with baptism.

> *But thanks be to God that, though you were once slaves of sin, you have become obedient from the heart to that form of teaching to which you were committed.*

When they obeyed from the heart that form of doctrine, which in this context is baptism, they were freed from the slavery of sin. To obey that form of doctrine is to obey the gospel.

Remember the eunuch in **Acts 8**? The eunuch asked, *"What prevents me from being baptized?"* Philip said that if he believed with all his heart, he could. *"I believe,"* the eunuch replied. He wholeheartedly obeyed the form of doctrine and the gospel, being baptized in water.

On the day of Pentecost, Luke recorded these words:
> Then those who accepted his word were baptized, and about three thousand were added to their number that day. **Acts 2:41**

These three thousand people obeyed the gospel by being baptized. We read:
> The word of God increased, and the number of disciples multiplied in Jerusalem, and a great many priests became obedient to the faith. **Acts 6:7**

These many priests obeyed the faith, obeyed the gospel by being baptized, because everywhere the same plan of God was followed.

In **Acts 8**, besides the eunuch, we have the conversion of the Samaritans.

> *But when they believed Philip as he preached the good news about the kingdom of God and the name of Jesus Christ, they were baptized, both men and women.* **Acts 8:12**

The Samaritans obeyed the gospel by being baptized.

In **Acts 9** we read about Saul.

> *Immediately something like scales fell from his eyes, and he could see again. Then he got up and was baptized.* **Acts 9:18**

Paul got up and obeyed the gospel by being baptized.

In **Acts 10**, Cornelius and all his household heard the gospel and Peter said:

> *Can anyone withhold water from these people, who have received the Holy Spirit just as we have, and should not be baptized? And he commanded them to be baptized in the name of Jesus Christ. Then they asked him to stay with them for a few days.* **Acts 10:47-48**

Peter commanded and they obeyed the gospel by being baptized in water.

We also read about Lydia.

> *A woman named Lydia, from the city of Thyatira, a seller of purple cloth and a devout worshiper, listened to us. The Lord opened her heart to respond to what Paul was saying. After she was baptized, she and her entire household...* **Acts 16:14-15**

Lydia and everyone in her house obeyed the gospel by being baptized.

We also have the story of the jailer and his conversion.

> *That same hour of the night, as he was tending them, he washed their stripes from the scourging. Then he was baptized, along with all his family.* **Acts 16:33**

The jailer and all his family obeyed the gospel and were baptized that very hour of the night.

Finally, we have the conversion of the Corinthians:

> *But Crispus, the ruler of the synagogue, believed in the Lord with all his house: and many of the*

Corinthians also, when they heard it, believed, and were baptized. **Acts 18:8**

Many of the Corinthians obeyed the gospel. They were baptized.

Conclusion

I posed the question, and we will answer it according to the Bible. "How can anyone obey the gospel?" The biblical answer is by dying as Christ died, being buried in the waters of baptism as a figure of Christ's burial and being resurrected from the waters to walk in newness of life. We respond with many biblical examples. To obey the gospel is to be baptized as the Bible commands.

The second question for you is:
"Have you obeyed the gospel as the Bible teaches?"

This is a question I cannot answer. Only you can.
"Have you been baptized for the forgiveness of your sins?"

In the next chapter we will continue to look at what the Bible says about the purpose of baptism.

Chapter 4
What is the Purpose of Baptism? (2)

Other Scriptures About the Necessity of Baptism

Sometimes it seems that there are few verses dealing with baptism because it is rarely discussed in churches. However, this impression is false. The term appears 21 times as a noun in the ARA version and about 80 times as a verb, totaling over 100 occurrences. It is a topic that should not be neglected. Let us examine some more of these passages; but let us do so by answering the following question...

What happens at baptism?

We must remember that the letters were written to saints in different places and congregations. While the churches in Galatia were experiencing great troubles, Paul wrote to them as brothers in Christ. To them and others, Paul speaks of baptism in the past tense, because they had already been baptized.

Paul says the following about baptism.

For as many of you as were baptized into Christ have clothed yourselves with Christ. **Galatians 3:27**

The Purpose of Baptism (part 2)
At baptism we are clothed with Christ!

Baptism

1 **Galatians 3:26-27**
For you are all sons of God through faith in Christ Jesus. For as many of you as were baptized into Christ have put on Christ.

2 **Ephesians 4:22**
that you put off, concerning your former conduct, the old man which grows corrupt according to the deceitful lusts,

3 **Ephesians 4:23**
and be renewed in the spirit of your mind,

4 **Ephesians 4:24**
and that you put on the new man which was created according to God, in true righteousness and holiness.

Paul speaks of putting on Christ or the new man in diverse passages. For example:

> *The night is far spent, the day is at hand. Therefore, let us cast off the works of darkness and put on the armor of light. Let us walk properly, as in the daytime, not in revelry and drunkenness, not in sexual immorality and wantonness, not in strife and envying. But put on the Lord Jesus Christ, and make no provision for the flesh, to fulfill its desires.* **Romans 13:12-14**

We leave the old clothes of our lives in the past and put on new clothes: Christ himself. Paul continues:

> *that ye put off, concerning your former conversation, the old man, which is corrupt according to the deceitful lusts; and be renewed in the spirit of your mind; and that ye put on the new man, created after God in true righteousness and holiness.* **Ephesians 4:22-24**

Paul also says:

> *Do not lie to one another, since you have put off the old man with his deeds and have put on the new man who is being renewed in knowledge according to the image of his Creator.* **Colossians 3: 9-10**

This new man we must put on is Jesus. When does this happen? According to Paul in **Galatians 3:27,** when we are baptized. What happens in baptism? We are clothed with Christ.

We have already studied Paul's conversion, but since we are exploring the question of baptism, let us look at that passage again. Ananias said to Paul.

> And now why do you delay? Get up, be baptized, and wash away your sins, calling on his name. **Acts 22:16**

What happens at baptism? Our sins are washed away.

Peter responded to those who wanted to know what to do and said:

> Repent and be baptized every one of you in the name of Jesus Christ for the remission of sins, and you will receive the gift of the Holy Spirit. **Acts 2:38**

What happens at baptism? We receive the remission (forgiveness) of sins and the gift of the Holy Spirit.

Again, Paul wrote:

> Or do you not know that all of us who were baptized into Christ Jesus were baptized into his death? We were therefore buried with him through

63

baptism into death, in order that, just as Christ was raised from the dead through the glory of the Father, we too might walk in newness of life. **Romans 6:3-4**

What happens in baptism? We are buried and united with Christ, but we are also raised with him to walk in newness of life. What happens in baptism? We are raised to begin our new life in Christ Jesus.

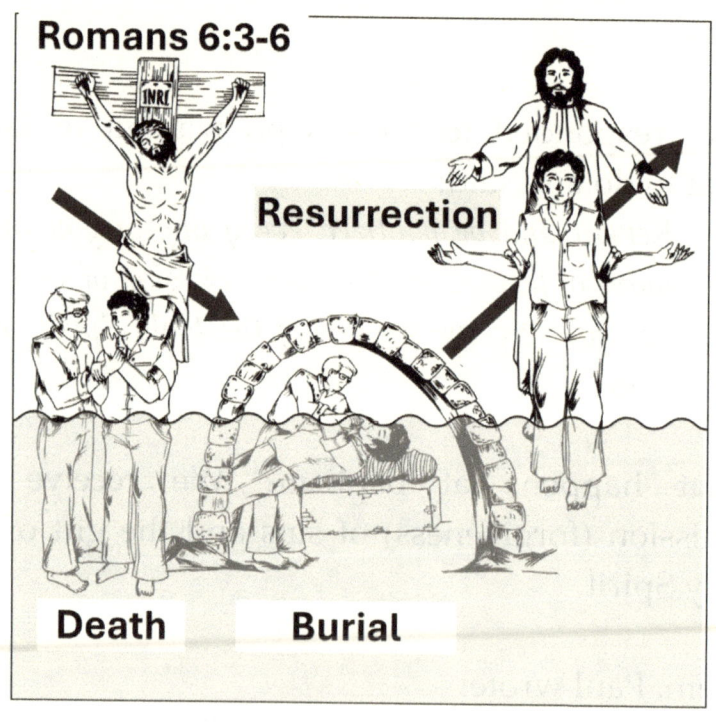

It is important to see what happens in baptism. Let us examine this verse.

For if we have been united together in the likeness of his death, certainly we shall also be in the likeness of his resurrection. **Romans 6:5**

The word "if" makes the phrase conditional. That means: *if* this condition exists, *then* we will have this result.

Let us understand this in context. The verb "we were" is in the past tense. He wrote this letter to those saved in Rome. Those who had already been baptized. The phrase "united with him in the likeness of his death" refers to baptism, considering verses **3-4**. The following verb is conjugated in the future tense, "we will be." And the final phrase of this passage, "in the likeness of his resurrection," is the future result we should expect. Since we are talking about a future resurrection, which we will receive, then this phrase refers to the final resurrection when Christ returns.

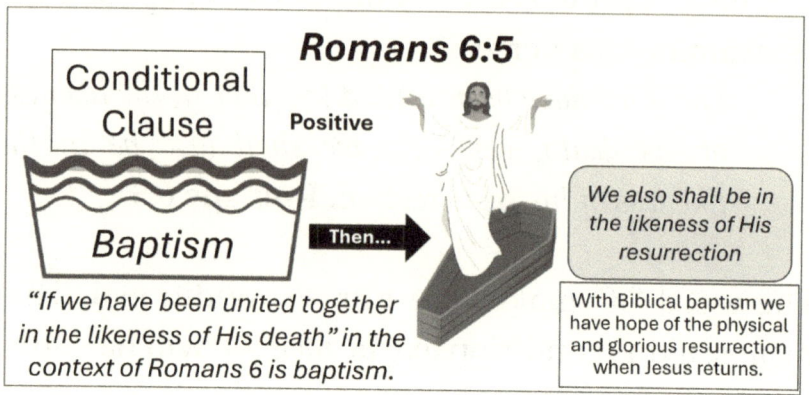

Romans 6:5

Conditional Clause

Positive

Baptism

Then...

We also shall be in the likeness of His resurrection

"If we have been united together in the likeness of His death" in the context of Romans 6 is baptism.

With Biblical baptism we have hope of the physical and glorious resurrection when Jesus returns.

Let me paraphrase this verse for a greater understanding. If we fulfill the condition of being united with Jesus in the likeness of his death, which in this context is baptism, certainly, in the future when Jesus returns, we will also be in the likeness of his resurrection, that is, we will be physically resurrected as Jesus physically emerged from the tomb. Everyone will emerge from the tombs (John **5:28-29**). But the baptized will emerge from the tombs to receive a new body as Christ received.

> *For our citizenship is in heaven, and from it we also eagerly wait for the Savior, the Lord Jesus Christ, who will transform our lowly body that it may be conformed to His glorious body, according to the working by which He is able even to subdue all things to Himself.* **Philippians 3:20-21**

The teaching of this verse about baptism should not be underestimated. What is Paul saying happens in baptism here? We are united with Christ and prepared for the final resurrection.

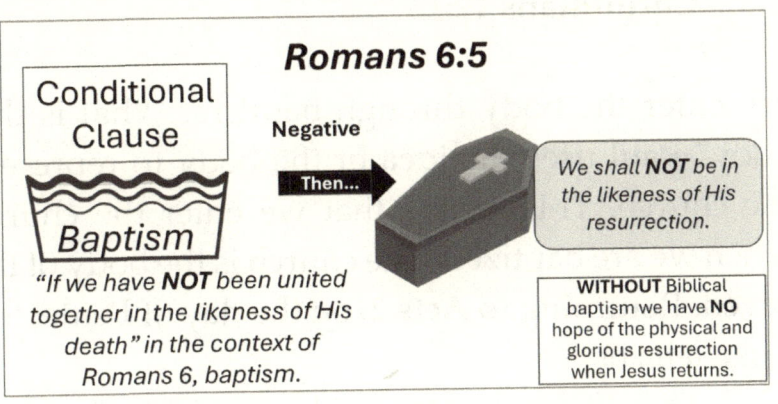

Still in this context, Paul said:

> *But thanks be to God that, though you were once slaves of sin, you became obedient from the heart to that form of teaching to which you were committed; and having been set free from sin, you became slaves of righteousness.* **Romans 6:17-18**

The context here concerns baptism. It is not possible that "obeying that form of teaching" is anything other than baptism.

So, what happens in baptism? When we obey the form of doctrine to which we have been delivered, we are freed from sin and made servants of righteousness.

Paul further talks about baptism in this passage.

> *For by one Spirit we were all baptized into one body—whether Jews or Greeks, slave or free—and were all made to drink of one Spirit.* **1 Corinthians 12:13**

We enter the body through baptism. What is this body? Paul uses the idea of the body to represent the church. This means that we enter the church when we are baptized. The church is the body of the saved. Returning to **Acts 2**, on the day of Pentecost, Luke tells us:

> *Then those who accepted his word were baptized, and about three thousand were added to their number that day.* **Acts 2:41**

What were they added to? This addition happened that day and every day after. In the New International Version we read:

> *praising God and enjoying the favor of all the people. And the Lord added to their number daily those who were being saved.* **Acts 2:47**

It is interesting how the King James and New King James versions present this verse like this.

> *Praising God. The whole city was moved with sympathy, and the Lord himself added to the*

church daily those who were being saved. **Acts 2:47**

What happens at baptism? We are added to the church. What is the church? The church is the body of all the saved.

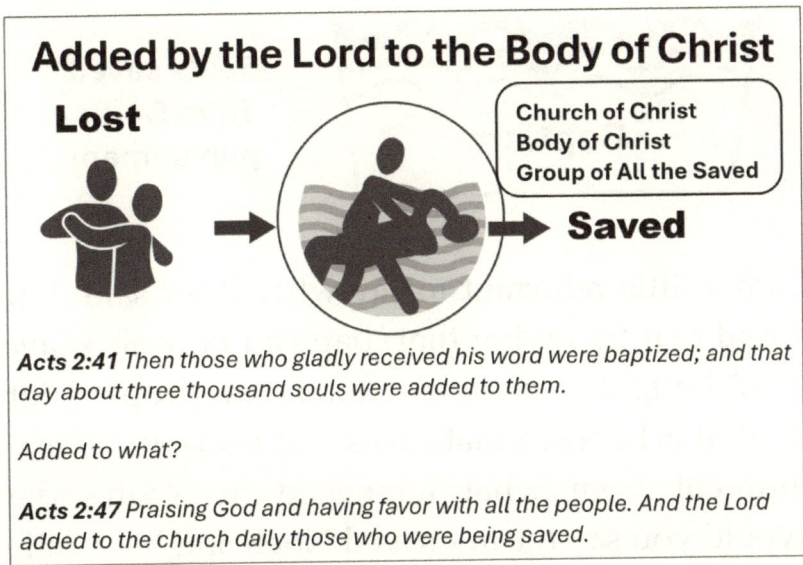

Added by the Lord to the Body of Christ

Lost

Church of Christ
Body of Christ
Group of All the Saved

Saved

Acts 2:41 Then those who gladly received his word were baptized; and that day about three thousand souls were added to them.

Added to what?

Acts 2:47 Praising God and having favor with all the people. And the Lord added to the church daily those who were being saved.

In his first letter, the apostle Peter also speaks of baptism. He compares it to the story of Noah and his family, who were saved from the Flood.

Eight people were saved, and Peter says:
> *… baptism, which is a type, now also saves you, not the removal of the filth of the flesh, but the answer of a good conscience toward God, through the resurrection of Jesus Christ.* **1 Peter 3:21**

8 souls saved
from God's
punishment

Souls saved
from God's
punishment

Baptism

I am a little reluctant to say what Peter said. I am afraid that by saying that "baptism now also saves you," I might be misunderstood, that people might think it is baptism that saves, not Jesus. But it is no different from what happened in Noah's day. Would you say the ark saved Noah and his family? Yes. But was it the ark, without God and without faith in God? Of course not! Baptism saves us because God commanded it; we do it, and our faith in God is fulfilled at that moment.

So, what happens at baptism? We are saved.

Paul has another passage about baptism besides **Romans 6:3-5**, where he also says that baptism symbolizes Christ's burial and resurrection. But in this passage, he adds more facts about baptism. Paul says:

> *In him you were also circumcised with a circumcision made without hands, by putting off the body of the sins of the flesh by the circumcision of Christ. You were buried with him in baptism, in which you were also raised with him through faith in the working of God, who raised him from the dead.* **Colossians 2:11-12**

For the Jews, circumcision was a physical mark proving that they were in covenant with God; that they were part of God's people. Here Paul says that in baptism we are circumcised, but not by human hands. It is as if we undergo spiritual surgery that marks us as God's people. Here too, he says it is "through faith in the working of God." There is no point in going into the water if you do not have faith in God. But with faith, He will take away your sins at that moment and make you His child. What happens in baptism? We are spiritually circumcised and made God's people.

Bible Verses That Don't Use the Word Baptism

People doubt that some of these verses refer to baptism, especially since they do not use the word.

But the teachings of these verses fit perfectly with the teachings of the verses already examined.

Jesus received Nicodemus at night. In his conversation with him, Jesus told him about the following.

> *Very truly I tell you, unless one is born of water and the Spirit, he cannot enter the kingdom of God.* **John 3:5**

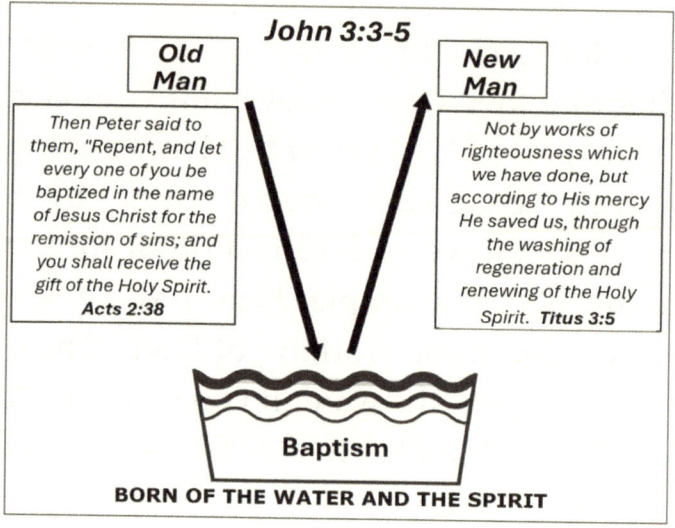

We can see two elements here in the new birth of man, that is, salvation to a new life. Water is the first element; and if it does not represent baptism, what does it represent? The second is the Holy Spirit; and who can deny that the Spirit is part of our transformation? See how this finds parallels in this example. Remember what Peter said?

Repent, every one of you, and be baptized in the name of Jesus for the remission [forgiveness] of your sins, and you will receive the gift of the Holy Spirit. **Acts 2:38**

water = baptism
born of the Spirit = gift of the Holy Spirit

Paul also makes a parallel in which he does not use the word baptism, but which becomes difficult to explain unless he is talking about baptism. In this passage Paul says:

not by works of righteousness which we have done, but according to his mercy he saved us, through the washing of regeneration and renewing of the Holy Spirit. **Titus 3:5**

Here the "washing of regeneration" must be baptism and the action of the Holy Spirit in our salvation and transformation is also present.

Another passage from Paul that refers to baptism indirectly is **Ephesians 2:5-6**. Here, Paul speaks of the moment we receive life:

And when we were dead in trespasses, made us alive together with Christ, by grace you have been saved, and raised us up together and seated us with him in the heavenly places in Christ Jesus.

When Paul speaks of our spiritual resurrection, he indicates that it happens when we are baptized. We have already seen this in **Colossians 2:12** and **Romans 6:4**. In **Ephesians 2:5-6**, which is a parallel passage to these two, Paul does not use the word baptism, but there is no reason to believe that he is not speaking of the moment of our baptism.

Some believe that **Ephesians 5:14** was an excerpt from a baptismal hymn.

> *Wherefore he says: Awake, O thou that sleepest, arise from the dead, and Christ shall give thee light.*

It is possible that here again we have a reference to baptism.

Paul also uses words that make it sound like he is talking about baptism.

Speaking about the church, he says:

> *that he might sanctify her, having cleansed her by the washing of water with the word.* **Ephesians 5:26**

> *For it is impossible for those who were once enlightened, and have tasted of the heavenly gift,*

and were made partakers of the Holy Spirit.
Hebrews 6:4

There are manuscript variations here: the Syriac and Ethiopic versions read "once baptized"; and the word is believed to be used in **Hebrews 10:32** also referring to baptism. Baptism was called "illumination" by the ancients, such as Justin Martyr and Clement of Alexandria [11]in the second century. We cannot be certain, but it would not be surprising to learn that they replaced the word "illuminated" with "baptized."

So? You already know the answer. – What happens at baptism?

What happens at baptism?

[11] https://www.crossroadsinitiative.com/media/articles/baptism-as-illumination-in-the-early-church/

Let us summarize what the Bible says in these 10 passages. Here are the benefits you receive when you are baptized.

1. **Galatians 3:27** We are clothed with Christ.
2. **Acts 22:16** Our sins are washed away.
3. **Acts 2:38** We have received the forgiveness of sins and the gift of the Holy Spirit.
4. **Romans 6:3-4** We are resurrected to begin our new life in Christ Jesus.
5. **Romans 6:5** We are united with Christ and prepared for the final resurrection.
6. **Romans 6:17-18** We are freed from sin and made servants of righteousness.
7. **1 Corinthians 12:13; Acts 2:41** We are added to the church, the body of the saved.
8. **1 Peter 3:21** We are saved.
9. **Colossians 2:11-12** We are spiritually circumcised, we are made people of God.
10. **John 3:5** We are born again: of water and the Spirit.

Now you know how to answer the question: What happens if I am not baptized?

If You Are Not Baptized

1. **Galatians 3:27** You are **NOT** clothed with Christ.
2. **Acts 22:16** Your sins are **NOT** washed away.
3. **Acts 2:38** You have **NOT** received the forgiveness of sins and the gift of the Holy Spirit.
4. **Romans 6:3-4** You are **NOT** resurrected to begin our new life in Christ Jesus.
5. **Romans 6:5** You are **NOT** united with Christ and prepared for the final resurrection.
6. **Romans 6:17** You are **NOT** freed from sin and made slaves of righteousness.
7. **1 Corinthians 12:13; Acts 2:41** You are **NOT** added to the church, the body of the saved.
8. **1 Peter 3:21** You are **NOT** saved.
9. **Colossians 2:11-12** You are **NOT** spiritually circumcised, and you are **NOT** made a part of God's people.
10. **John 3:5** You are **NOT** born again of water and the Spirit and are **NOT** in the kingdom of God.

Conclusion

Baptism by immersion in water of the penitent believer ready to follow Jesus is essential for salvation. I am not saying that. That is what the Bible says.

Have you been baptized for the forgiveness of your sins?

Chapter 5
Who Should Be Baptized and When?

Who should be baptized?

Obviously, in the last chapter, we showed that the Bible teaches us that anyone who wants to be saved must, among other things, be baptized. But in this chapter, it is better to ask: Who is a candidate for baptism?

Remember what Peter said at the end of his sermon on the day of Pentecost? **Acts 2:38** "Repent and let every one of you be baptized." A person who is not penitent of his sins is not a candidate for baptism.

Luke also spoke of those baptized on the day of Pentecost. **Acts 2:41** states, "...those who accepted his word were baptized..." This means that to be baptized, one must first hear and accept the message of salvation, the gospel of Jesus. If one does not accept the message, one should not be baptized. Baptism is not to be forced on anyone. Baptism comes with a person's decision to accept the message and the Lordship of Jesus.

When they arrived in Brazil, the Catholics baptized (sprinkled) the Indians, who did not even understand the priests' language, Portuguese. The Indians did not accept the message. In fact, they did not even repent—and how could they repent without even understanding the message that speaks of the need for repentance?

Should children be baptized or do they need to be baptized?

Both Catholics and some evangelical churches baptize children. Can a child repent? Do these baptized babies understand the message of the Gospel? Do they understand what sin is? Can they repent of their sins? Do they even have sins?

The Bible does not have an example of a child being baptized. Jesus taught that they are pure and innocent and therefore saved. Jesus says:

Let the little children come to me, and do not hinder them, for the kingdom of heaven belongs to such as these. **Matthew 19:14**

Innocents!

Jesus had already said:
Truly I tell you, unless you change and become like little children, you will never enter the kingdom of heaven. **Matthew 18:3**

Innocents!

There is a principle of responsibility for one's own actions in the Bible. Consider that some people think of the original sin of Adam and Eve, saying that every human being inherits this sin from Adam and is born already needing to be saved from it.

However the Bible teaches us that children will not be punished for the sins of their parents.
But you say, 'Why does not the son bear the iniquity of the father?' Because the son did what was right and just, and kept all my statutes and did them, he will surely live. The soul who sins will die. The son will not bear the iniquity of the father, nor the father the iniquity of the son. The righteousness of the righteous will be on him, and

the wickedness of the wicked will be on him.
Ezekiel 18:19-20

The son does not bear the father's sin. The son does not suffer the punishment for what the father did.

The apostle Paul speaks about gaining a new life and why we need it.

He gave you life, who were dead in trespasses and sins. **Ephesians 2:1**

Did Paul say that Christ gave them life because they were dead in the trespasses and sins of Adam? Did Paul say that they received life from Jesus because they were dead due to the sins of their parents? No, Paul said that they were dead in their own trespasses and sins, and that Jesus Christ gave them life. Responsibility is individual.

So, how old does one have to be to be baptized?

Well, one must have come to understand sin and that one is a lost sinner. It requires a certain individual responsibility. One must be able to grasp the message of the gospel. Every child is different. Each child develops at a different pace. There are even special people who never reach the "age of reason." I believe the Bible does not give us a specific age due to the differences between each of us. Parents of minors must be attentive and instruct their children about God and the things of God. And when they reach around 10, 11, or 12 years old, they will be able to understand and make responsible decisions.

Luke also recorded this.

> *But when they believed Philip as he preached the good news about the kingdom of God and the name of Jesus Christ, they were baptized.* **Acts 8:12**

You must accept the message, believe it, before you can be baptized. Philip told the eunuch he was evangelizing in **Acts 8:37** when he asked for baptism: "...if you **believe with all your heart, you may**." And again, in **Acts 18:8**, Luke wrote: "...many of the Corinthians, **when they heard it, believed** and were baptized."

A person who has been baptized in the wrong way or for the wrong purpose should be baptized again.

Paul said in **Ephesians 4:5** that there is only one baptism, and therefore there is no need to be baptized again. Well, what Paul was saying is that there is only one valid baptism. Valid baptism must be done in the manner and for the purpose Jesus instructed. We have the case in **Acts 19** of twelve men who received incorrect instructions about baptism and were baptized (immersed). The apostle Paul asked them:

> *Did you receive the Holy Spirit when you believed? They answered, No, we have not even heard that there is a Holy Spirit.* **Acts 19:2**

The baptism that Peter had been teaching since the day of Pentecost included forgiveness and the gift of the Holy Spirit (**Acts 2:38**). Paul was surprised by these words and continued asking:

> *Then what baptism did you receive? They answered, The baptism of John.* **Acts 19:3**

It was not the baptism of Jesus, in the name of Jesus; in the name of the Father and of the Son and of the Holy Spirit, to receive forgiveness of sins and the gift of the Holy Spirit. Paul then explains to them:

> *John's baptism was a baptism of repentance. He told the people to believe in the one who would come after him, that is, in Jesus.* **Acts 19:4**

What should be the reaction of someone who has received the wrong baptism?

> *When they heard this, they were baptized in the name of the Lord Jesus.* **Acts 19:5**

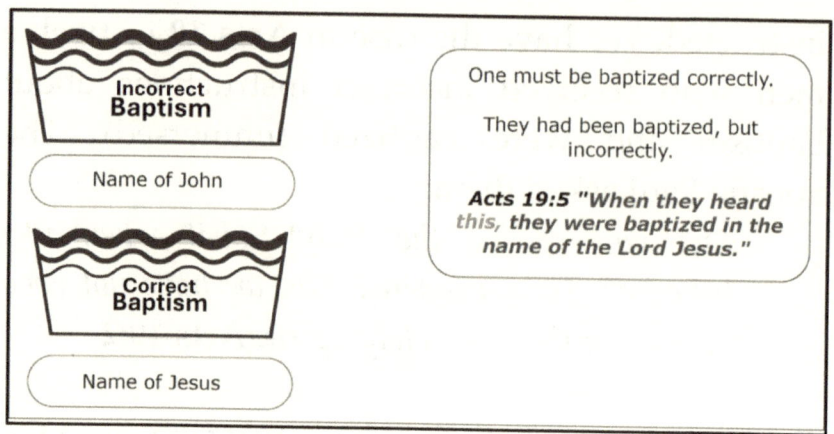

If you were baptized incorrectly, for the wrong purpose, or in the wrong way, you must correct this error by being baptized in the right way and for the right purpose.

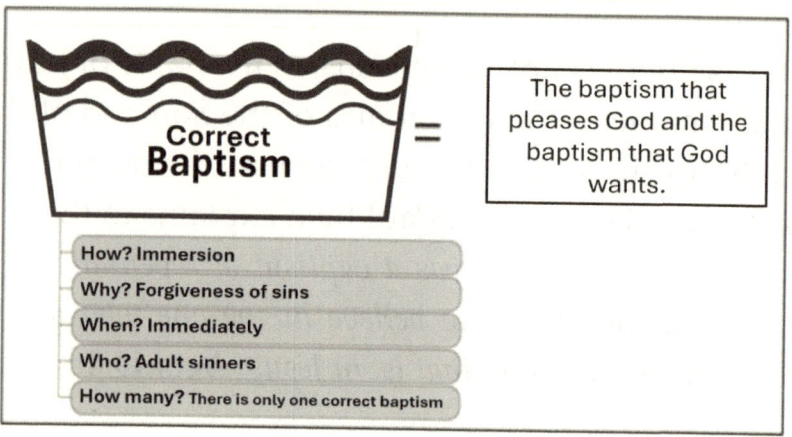

Do you want to stand before God someday and explain to Him why, knowing you were baptized the wrong way or for the wrong purpose, you did not correct your mistake? I hope you have a good excuse, but I cannot imagine what would work.

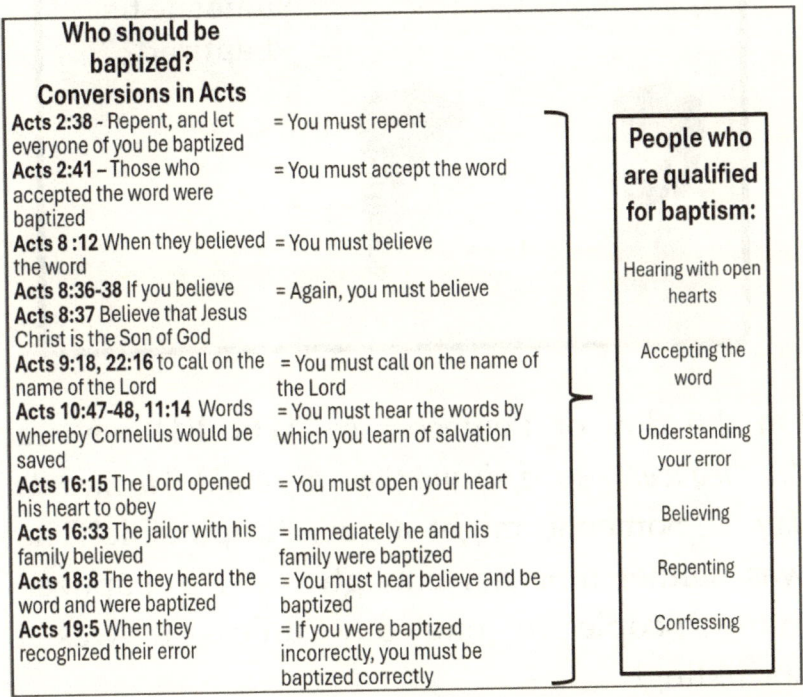

Who should be baptized?
Conversions in Acts

Acts 2:38 - Repent, and let everyone of you be baptized	= You must repent
Acts 2:41 – Those who accepted the word were baptized	= You must accept the word
Acts 8 :12 When they believed the word	= You must believe
Acts 8:36-38 If you believe	= Again, you must believe
Acts 8:37 Believe that Jesus Christ is the Son of God	
Acts 9:18, 22:16 to call on the name of the Lord	= You must call on the name of the Lord
Acts 10:47-48, 11:14 Words whereby Cornelius would be saved	= You must hear the words by which you learn of salvation
Acts 16:15 The Lord opened his heart to obey	= You must open your heart
Acts 16:33 The jailor with his family believed	= Immediately he and his family were baptized
Acts 18:8 The they heard the word and were baptized	= You must hear believe and be baptized
Acts 19:5 When they recognized their error	= If you were baptized incorrectly, you must be baptized correctly

People who are qualified for baptism:

Hearing with open hearts

Accepting the word

Understanding your error

Believing

Repenting

Confessing

Unfortunately, even in denominations that immerse in water as the Bible commands, there are many that do not believe in the fundamental essence of baptism for salvation. For that reason, they delay days, weeks, months, or even years before allowing someone to be baptized. Let us allow the Scriptures to speak to and answer this question.

On the day of Pentecost in **Acts 2:41** we read: *"...they were baptized; and there were added to them that day..."* Someone might argue, "Impossible! There was neither time nor enough water to baptize so many people in one day unless it was by sprinkling!"

Jerusalem was a big city and there were *mikvahs*[12] and fountains scattered throughout the

---

[12] A *mikvah* is a type of tank or pool for ritual immersion in water used in Judaism to achieve ritual purity. Archaeologists have discovered more than 125 *mikvahs*. near the Temple Mount, many of them along a main road leading to the southern entrance. Jewish men and women sang Ascension Psalms as they walked to the Temple. They would purify themselves for worship by immersing themselves in one of the *mikvahs* near the main entrance. Jesus, as a Jew, would have used these same microphones before entering the Temple area. Paul certainly would have used them, especially on his last visit in Acts 21:26, when "he purified himself...and went into the temple."

city. Also remember that, although it would be difficult for one person to baptize three thousand others, the twelve apostles were there at that time (**Acts 2:14**). The preaching began at 8 or 9 a.m., so there was more than enough time to baptize three thousand people.

Paul certainly would have used them, especially on his last visit in **Acts 21:26**, when *"he purified himself...and went into the temple."*

But the point here really is that those immersed on the day of Pentecost in Acts 2 were immersed on the same day, immediately.

The Samaritans were also baptized as soon as they believed.
> *But when they believed..., they were baptized...*
> **Acts 8:12**

This means that when they believed in the message and they were baptized.

The Ethiopian eunuch asked to be baptized immediately. He said:

---

http://www.knollwoodchurch.org/yr2018/b22_baptize_3000.html

*...look, here is water, **what hinders** me from being baptized? ...and Philip **baptized** the eunuch.* **Acts 8:35-38**

Paul waited three days to be baptized. Even so, when Ananias arrived and told him he should be baptized, he did not delay any longer. We cannot expect someone to want to be baptized without knowing the necessity of baptism.

*Why are you waiting?... then he arose and **was baptized.** **Acts 9:9,17-18 (22:16)***

Peter ordered that Cornelius and his entire household be baptized in water, and we can understand that it was something immediate.

*And he commanded **them to be baptized** in the name of Jesus Christ.* **Acts 10:44-48**

Look at the case of Lydia and her household in **Acts 16:13-15.**

The phrase *"**after being baptized** ..."* indicates that there was no delay.

Also, the jailer, as we have seen did this.

... that very hour of the night... he was baptized, and all his household. **Acts 16:30-33**

*...many of the Corinthians, when they heard it, believed **and were baptized**. Acts 18:8*

This seems to have been immediately. In all the cases mentioned, the baptism of those who heard and believed the gospel took place during the preachers' first contact with their listeners. Most of them were Jews, but not all.

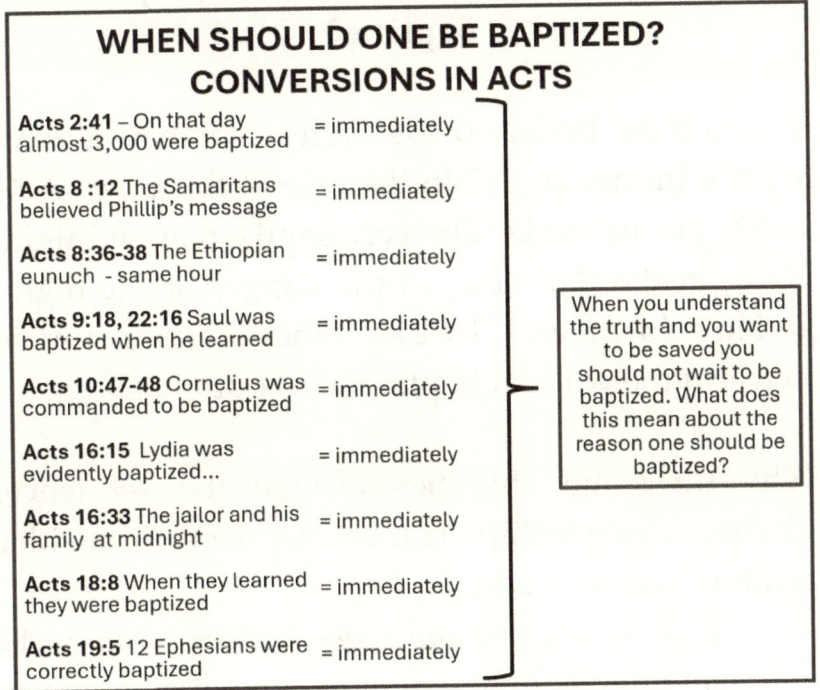

WHEN SHOULD ONE BE BAPTIZED?
CONVERSIONS IN ACTS

Acts 2:41 – On that day almost 3,000 were baptized = immediately

Acts 8:12 The Samaritans believed Phillip's message = immediately

Acts 8:36-38 The Ethiopian eunuch - same hour = immediately

Acts 9:18, 22:16 Saul was baptized when he learned = immediately

Acts 10:47-48 Cornelius was commanded to be baptized = immediately

Acts 16:15 Lydia was evidently baptized... = immediately

Acts 16:33 The jailor and his family at midnight = immediately

Acts 18:8 When they learned they were baptized = immediately

Acts 19:5 12 Ephesians were correctly baptized = immediately

When you understand the truth and you want to be saved you should not wait to be baptized. What does this mean about the reason one should be baptized?

What justifies such urgency?

Perhaps, considering the Bible, the answer is the answer to another question.

When is someone saved?

When should someone be baptized? Immediately upon wanting to be saved! It was always this way in the Bible. There was never a delay in the biblical examples, as the person understood baptism according to God's will.

What does this indicate about the purpose of baptism?

It would be better to ask: Why did they always baptize immediately? In the case of the jailer (**Acts 16:33**), he and his family were baptized at midnight. Wow, in the darkness, in the danger of the night, and in cold water! Why didn't they wait for sunrise to warm the water if baptism was optional?

Why do some churches change the sequence, placing discipleship before baptism? Consider again what Jesus said.

> *Then Jesus came and spoke to them, saying, All authority has been given to me in heaven and on earth. Go therefore and make disciples of all nations, baptizing them in the name of the Father and of the Son and of the Holy Spirit, teaching them to observe all that I have commanded you.*

And surely I am with you always, to the very end of the age. **Matthew 28:18-20.**

Making disciples: Jesus commanded; therefore, we must teach. What did he say we should do after baptizing in the name of the Father and of the Son and of the Holy Spirit? What comes next?

> *... teaching them to observe all things whatsoever I have commanded you.* **Matthew 28:20**

What often happens in churches is the opposite. They teach everything (that the pastor sees fit to teach) before baptizing. Why? Because they consider that those who raise their hand, accept Jesus, invite Him into their heart, pray the sinner's prayer, or something similar, are already saved without baptism. But these things—like raising one's hand, accepting Jesus, inviting Him into one's heart, or praying the sinner's prayer—are not found in the Bible. In the Bible, baptism is the moment of salvation and happens immediately when someone wants to be baptized.

What is your practice? Shouldn't it be the same as what is taught in the Bible?

Conclusion

Who should be baptized and when?

Anyone who wants to be saved and follow Jesus to their heavenly home must be baptized immediately. They must have faith in Jesus and his message, obey the gospel, repent of their sins, and confess Jesus as their Lord. It is impossible to have Jesus as their savior without accepting him as their owner and being baptized (immersed) in water by God's authority for the forgiveness of sins and to receive the gift of the Holy Spirit. Thus, once saved, one must continue to serve Jesus faithfully until death. As John said:

> *Be faithful until death, and I will give you the crown of life.* **Revelation 2:10b**

Have you done this?

Do you want to be saved?

Chapter 6
Objections to Baptism

"The Bible teaches that we are saved by faith alone."

The problem with today's "faith-alone" proponents of salvation is that they have created a false and unbiblical definition of "faith." Their original statement, "salvation is by faith alone," is a perfectly valid biblical argument. But salvation by faith alone does not preclude baptism—it requires it. If you truly have faith in Jesus, you will trust and obey what he commands. Jesus said, "He who believes and is baptized will be saved." Baptism does not diminish salvation by faith alone—it confirms your faith in Christ's word.

We are saved by faith	When we don't obey, we don't have faith, and we are not saved
Hebrews 11:4 By faith Abel offered	If Abel had refused to offer, he would not have had faith.
Hebrews 11:5 By faith Enoch pleased God	If Enoch had not pleased God, he would not have had faith
Hebrews 11:7 By faith Noah prepared an ark	If Noah had not prepared the ark he would not have had faith
Hebrews 11:8 By Faith Abraham obeyed	If Abraham had not obeyed, he would not have had faith

"The Bible teaches that we are saved by grace and not by works; baptism is a work, therefore baptism cannot be required for salvation."

The problem here is also the definition, not of the word "grace," but of the word "work." Again, based on its original premise, salvation by grace is a perfectly valid biblical argument.

Salvation by grace does not preclude baptism, because baptism is not a meritorious work. "Grace" means that we receive what we do not deserve. If I teach that baptism makes me worthy of salvation, I am wrong. I do not teach this as some claim. Nothing can make a sinner worthy of salvation.

Does your faith (necessary for salvation) make you worthy of salvation? No!

Does repentance of your sins (necessary for salvation) make you worthy of salvation? No!

Your confession of Jesus as Lord (necessary for salvation, **Romans 10:9**) does not make you worthy of salvation.

To say that faith, repentance, or confession make you worthy of salvation would be to transform these actions into meritorious works. We cannot do that!

If anyone teaches that baptism makes a person worthy of salvation, I will be the first to condemn such teaching. Faith, repentance, confession, and baptism are necessary, but they do not nullify grace. We would only nullify grace if we taught that baptism is a meritorious work.

What transforms a person into someone who deserves salvation?

Ephesians 2:8 For by grace you have been saved through faith, and that not of yourselves; *it is* the gift of God,

- Does your faith transform you into someone who deserves salvation? No! But you must have faith to be saved.
- Does repenting of your sins make you worthy of salvation? No! But you must repent to be saved.
- Does confessing Jesus as Lord cause you to merit salvation? No! But you must confess Jesus to be saved.
- Does baptism make you deserving of salvation? No! But you must be baptized to be saved.
- Does following Jesus faithfully mean you merit salvation? No! But you must follow Jesus faithfully to be saved.

We are saved by grace and nothing we do or believe can make us worthy of salvation.
1 Peter 2:24 who Himself bore our sins in His own body on the tree, that we, having died to sins, might live for righteousness—by whose stripes you were healed.
Our part is obedient faith and by that alone God extends to us His grace.
Even with obedient faith we are sinners and merit punishment.
Romans 6:23 "For the wages of sin *is* death, but the gift of God *is* eternal life in Christ Jesus our Lord."
What transforms a person into someone who deserves salvation? NOTHING!

"The thief on the cross was not baptized."

He could have been baptized with the baptism of John the Baptist. (see **Matthew 3:5-6**) Many people were baptized by him. He certainly was not baptized with the baptism of Jesus, for Jesus only commanded his baptism on the day he ascended to heaven. **(Acts 1:2, Mark 16:19)**

Jesus lived his entire life under the Old Covenant, except for the 40 days **(Acts 1:3)** he lived on earth after his resurrection. The New Covenant began when Jesus died on the cross **(Matthew 26:28)**. Jesus gave his final commandments, including baptism, on the day he ascended to heaven **(Acts 1:2; Matthew 28:19-20; Mark 16:15-16)**. Therefore, the thief died under the Old Covenant before Jesus commanded his baptism, but we live under the New Covenant.

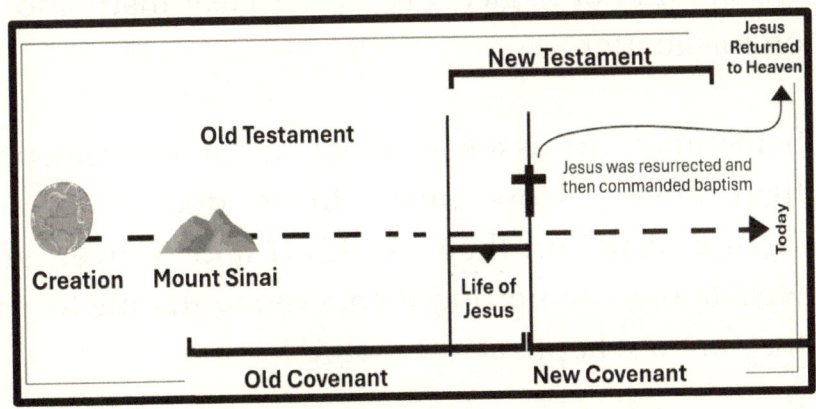

"What about people on their deathbed who have no way of being baptized? Will they be lost?"

I will not judge someone who wants to be baptized but finds themselves prevented in some way. I will not judge them. What I mean is, I will not say the person is saved, but I will not say they are lost either. My ministry is to teach what the Bible says. It is not to judge anyone's destiny. (**Acts 17:31**) This objection does not change the truth of what the Bible says.

I will not say there are exceptions to the rule, but in the hypothesis presented, the person who puts forward this idea might wonder: can exceptions become the rule for everyone? No. We live by the rule, and if God, in his grace and mercy, wants to make an exception to biblical instruction, he can; of course he can. But we are not in this situation, and we should not neglect our Lord's clear instructions on this matter.

Sometimes the issue is more about convenience than illness. How many times does someone "accept Jesus" on their deathbed and recover, get well, and go home; and then, even with time to act, they are not baptized afterward?

A missionary once visited a patient who was on his deathbed, and the man, already thinking he was going to die, wanted to be baptized. The missionary spoke to a nurse, went to the laundry room, found a tank on wheels, filled it with water, took it to the patient's hospital room, and baptized him in Christ Jesus. For convenience's sake, it would have been too easy to say, "He cannot. Let us leave him in God's hands. God will be fair."

It turns out that in this case; the man did not die. God heard the brothers' prayers, and he left the hospital healed. I am not suggesting that baptism healed him, but I am saying that when we want to do God's will, God will often show us the way.

"I can't be baptized because I live with someone, and we're not married."

I agree. You cannot be baptized. The truth is, if you are living with someone who is not your spouse, without being married, you are living in sin. And anyone who deliberately lives in sin is not saved and cannot be saved without repenting of their sins. In other words: Stop living in sin!

As we have seen in another Chapter, the candidate for baptism must repent of his sins. Jesus' first sermon was:

> Repent, for the kingdom of heaven is at hand. **Matthew 4:17**

Just before returning to heaven, he expressed his wish saying:

> And so, it is written, that the Christ should suffer, and on the third day rise from the dead, and that repentance and forgiveness of sins should be preached in his name to all nations, beginning from Jerusalem. **Luke 24:46-47**

Let me put it clearly. Anyone who is living in a state of constant sin is lost. They need to be baptized, yes, but if they continue to live in sin without repenting of their sins, they cannot be baptized; they cannot be saved.

In Brazil I heard of "church authorities" who would say in these situations that the couple could be saved without baptism, but they cannot be baptized, take the Lord's Supper or participate in other church activities until they obtain a marriage certificate from the registry office.

Forgive me for saying this, but this is a notion full of errors. Where in the Bible do you find this? And I confess that sometimes I question the pastors' reason for making this statement. People cannot take communion, but do they prevent people in this condition from tithing? Could they be trying to circumvent biblical teaching? It is as if they were saying, "You can't be a brother, but we let you be a saved 'half-brother' without baptism."

The biggest problem is the deception. People living in sin are deceived into believing they are saved, when in fact, without repentance and baptism, no one can be saved.

> *Peter said to them, 'Repent and be baptized every one of you in the name of Jesus Christ for the forgiveness of sins, and you will receive the gift of the Holy Spirit.* **Acts 2:38**

"When Paul said that 'there is one baptism' in Ephesians 4:5, wasn't he referring to the baptism of the Holy Spirit? If so then water baptism is no longer necessary."

First, the Bible ignores the "baptism *of the* Holy Spirit." The Bible nowhere mentions that the Holy Spirit baptizes anyone. That baptism was baptism with or in the Holy Spirit. Jesus told his disciples:

And as he was eating with them, he commanded them not to depart from Jerusalem, but to wait for the promise of the Father, which, he said, you heard from me. For John truly baptized with water, but you will be baptized with the Holy Spirit not many days from now. **Acts 1:4-5**

Notice this text: "Then I remembered the word of the Lord, how he said, 'John indeed baptized with water, but you will be baptized with the Holy Spirit.'" It does not say "by the Holy Spirit."

In **Acts 11:16** it also says "with" the Holy Spirit. It is not "of" or "by" the Holy Spirit.

Second, what happened on the day of Pentecost was the baptism with the Holy Spirit. If it had already happened, what was the baptism that the apostle Peter commanded in **Acts 2:38?** And if after the day of Pentecost, water baptism was no longer valid, why did Philip and the eunuch go into the water and Philip baptize him? **Acts 8:38.** And if the baptism with the Holy Spirit was the one baptism Paul mentioned in **Ephesians 4:5**, why did Peter command Cornelius and his entire household to be baptized in water? **Acts 10:47-48**

I cannot go into an extensive study now of the baptism with the Holy Spirit. It is not our topic. The baptism with the Holy Spirit deserves in-depth study. But **Ephesians 4:5** can only refer to the water baptism commanded by Jesus and taught and practiced to the end. **Matthew 28:19-20**

"But I have already been baptized! Are you telling me I need to be baptized again?"

First, were you immersed in water? If you were sprinkled, you were not baptized. If water was poured on your head, you were not baptized. I suggest revisiting Chapter 2, where we explored the meaning of the word in greater depth as Jesus used it.

Second, were you a child when you were baptized? Were you a repentant sinner? Or were you too young to understand these things?

Baptism is for people who have heard the gospel message, believed in Jesus, repented of their sins, and confessed Him as Lord. Baptism is for adults who consciously surrender their lives to Jesus. If you have not understood biblical baptism and acted accordingly, your baptism is not valid according to Scripture.

Third, did you think you were already saved when you decided to be baptized? If so, then why were you baptized?

Let us see what some people say to the question, "Why were you baptized?"

- "Well, I wanted to sing in the choir, but the pastor said I could not because I had not been baptized. So, I asked to be baptized."

- "I wanted to take the Lord's Supper, but the pastor said only baptized people could participate. So, I asked to be baptized."

- "I felt helpless without my church ID card. I asked the pastor for one, but he refused to give me one, saying I needed to be baptized first. And that's what I did."

- "The pastor said he wanted me to be a member of his church, but that I needed to be baptized to join. So, I was baptized.

None of this follows what the Bible teaches about why we should be baptized.

Were you saved before baptism? How was your salvation?

- "The pastor gave an appeal, and I raised my hand. He prayed and gave thanks to God for all who were saved by raising their hands that day."

- "The television evangelist asked me to pray the sinner's prayer, repeating what he said:
  'Heavenly Father, I know I am a sinner, and I deserve punishment. I believe that Jesus died on the cross for my sins. I now receive Him as my personal Lord and Savior. I promise to serve Him to the best of my ability. Please save me. In Jesus' name, amen.'

Then the pastor declared that all who repeated this prayer were saved.

- "I have been saved since birth. I was raised in a Christian home."

- "One day I was visiting a nearby church, and the pastor gave a very moving invitation that touched my heart. He invited everyone who wanted to be saved to come forward. I went to the front, he laid his hands on me and said a short prayer, thanking God for saving me that day."

Raising your hand is not wrong. Praying is not wrong. Expressing your desire to be saved is not wrong. What is wrong is saying someone is saved without having followed God's plan for salvation as revealed in the Bible. Failing to address the essential nature of baptism as part of God's plan of salvation is a serious omission.

There is only one legitimate baptism today. Paul said in **Ephesians 4:5** that *"there is one Lord, one faith, one baptism."* Of course, he was saying there is only one correct baptism. He also says there is only one Lord, but we know that in the world people serve the lords of power, fame, and money. What Paul was saying with this word "one" in this context is that there is only one that is only one correct or true Lord. Regarding baptism, there is only one that is right and valid. Today there are many baptisms taught but the only true and valid one is the one taught in the Bible.

If you received something called "baptism" but it was not done according to what the Bible says, you have not received Jesus' baptism. You need to receive the baptism Jesus commanded. "Ah, but now I know the truth about my baptism that I didn't know at the time. Now I know what I did and what happened. I was saved at that moment."

Have you ever taken the Lord's Supper? Yes. If someone comes in and takes the Lord's Supper without understanding what they are doing, is it valid? No. So how is it possible to be baptized correctly without understanding what is happening?

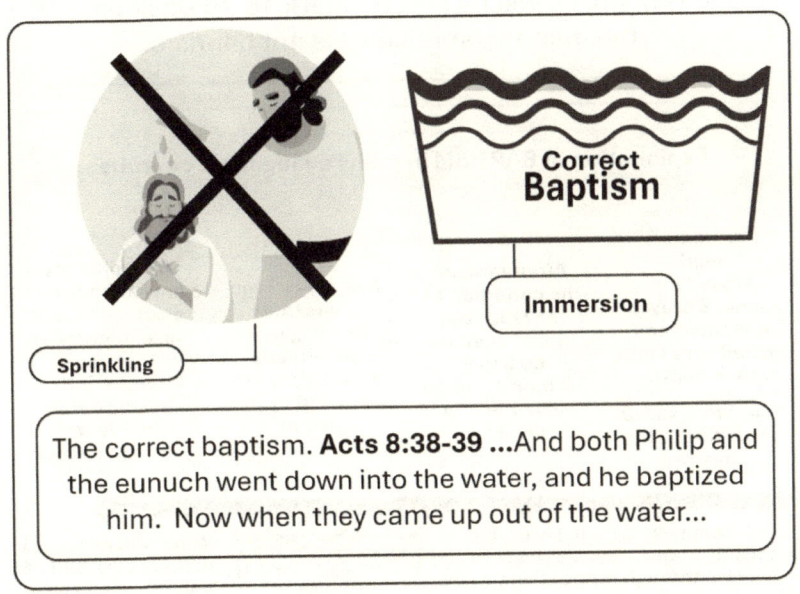

Sprinkling

Correct
Baptism

Immersion

The correct baptism. **Acts 8:38-39** ...And both Philip and the eunuch went down into the water, and he baptized him. Now when they came up out of the water...

I believe the objections have been answered with biblical teachings and clarity. If you disagree or have other arguments against the necessity of baptism for salvation, please contact us. Let us continue our dialogue.

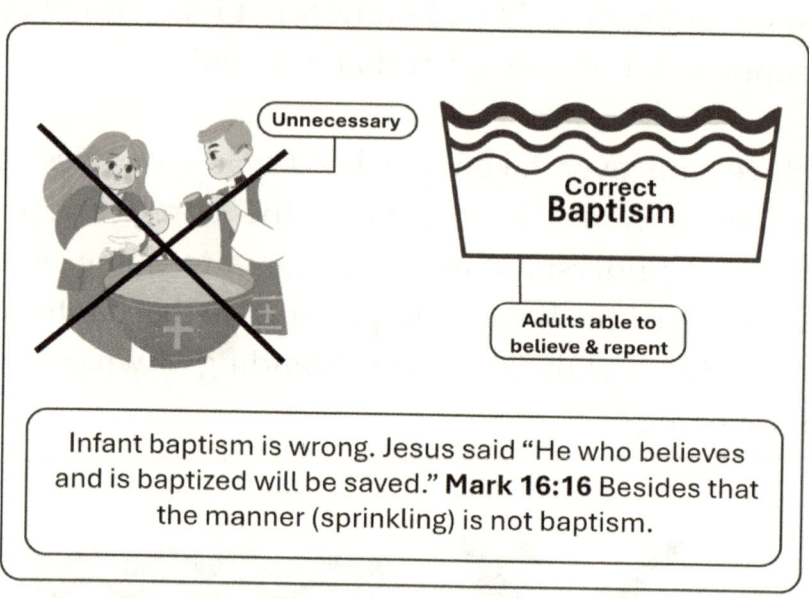

Infant baptism is wrong. Jesus said "He who believes and is baptized will be saved." **Mark 16:16** Besides that the manner (sprinkling) is not baptism.

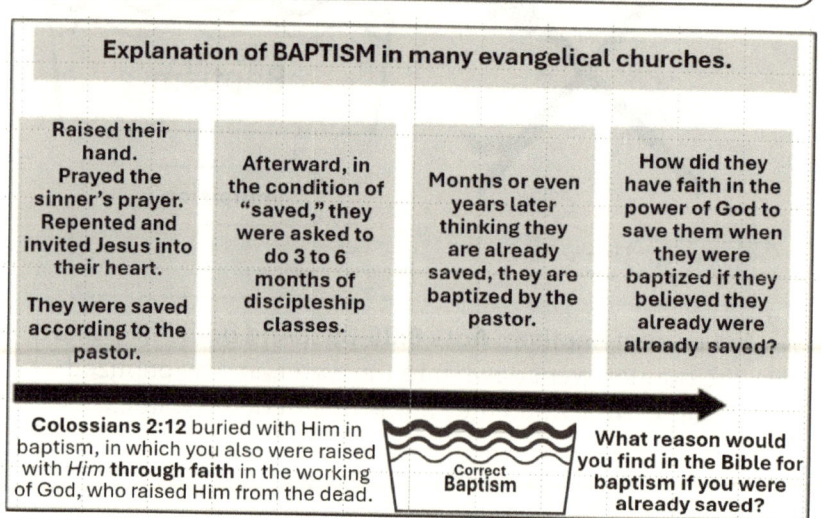

Explanation of BAPTISM in many evangelical churches.

Raised their hand. Prayed the sinner's prayer. Repented and invited Jesus into their heart.

They were saved according to the pastor.

Afterward, in the condition of "saved," they were asked to do 3 to 6 months of discipleship classes.

Months or even years later thinking they are already saved, they are baptized by the pastor.

How did they have faith in the power of God to save them when they were baptized if they believed they already were already saved?

Colossians 2:12 buried with Him in baptism, in which you also were raised with *Him* **through faith** in the working of God, who raised Him from the dead.

What reason would you find in the Bible for baptism if you were already saved?

Chapter 7
Baptism and Commitment

In the act of baptism, the person is making a commitment.

In F, LaGard Smith's book titled *Baptism: The Believer's Wedding Ceremony*, he presents baptism as a ceremony of marriage between the believer and Christ. Through the analogy of marriage, baptism is elevated to a personal proclamation of love and loyalty, through which true spiritual

conversion receives meaning and validity. His message about the need for faith and personal commitment provides the key to reestablishing a vibrant church in our time.

The Bible confirms that those who are baptized are making a commitment to Christ and His church. Just like the commitment of marriage, baptism should not be treated irresponsibly. As pointed out in other chapters of this book, baptism should not be treated recklessly. The religious world often fails to address the issue, and when it is addressed, it is often done outside the biblical context, within the context of human traditions and doctrines.

When someone is baptized, they are making a commitment to be a disciple of Christ. On the day Jesus was to return to heaven, 40 days after his resurrection, he gathered his eleven disciples, who would become his apostles, and gave them his final commands. (**Acts 1:2**) Matthew records this event this way:

> *Then the eleven disciples went away into Galilee, to the mountain which Jesus had appointed for them. When they saw Him, they worshiped Him; but some doubted. And Jesus came and spoke to them, saying, All authority has been given to Me in heaven and on earth. Go therefore and make disciples of all the nations, baptizing them in the name of the Father and of the Son and of the Holy Spirit, teaching them to observe all things that I have commanded you; and lo, I am with you always, even to the end of the age.' Amen.*
> **Matthew 28:16-20**

The eleven apostles needed to recognize Jesus' authority, and indeed, we all do. He has the right to command. He has all authority in heaven and on earth. When he commands, the disciple obeys.

The expression "make disciples" translates a single word in Greek, the verb μαθητεύω (*matheteuo*). This word means "to become a student/disciple, to make a disciple, to teach someone, to follow instructions from another, to be a committed student/learner."[2]

Making a disciple means committing someone to the teachings of that master—in this case, Jesus—and their initiation into Jesus' discipleship is baptism. Baptism is the disciple's moment of decision. However, they understand that there is still much to learn from the Master. And then comes the phrase that follows baptism: "teaching them to observe all things that I have commanded you."

Being a disciple of Jesus is a commitment to Jesus, but it is also a commitment to Jesus' teachings, beginning here with baptism. The decision to be saved is also marked by baptism. (**Mark 16:16**)[13] If we do not follow his teachings on baptism, is there any point in teaching "all things"?

---

[13] Mark also speaks of the moment of initiation, but he links it to salvation. The moment of becoming a disciple and being saved is the same: baptism.

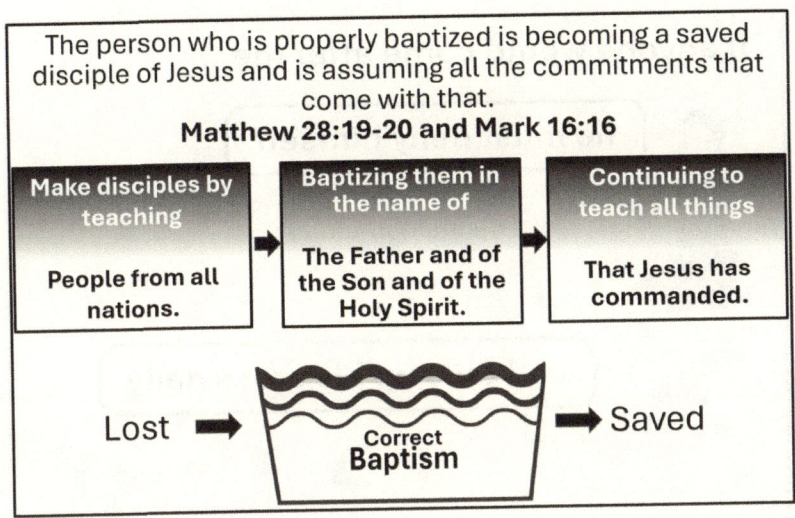

The person who is properly baptized is becoming a saved disciple of Jesus and is assuming all the commitments that come with that.
Matthew 28:19-20 and Mark 16:16

Make disciples by teaching	Baptizing them in the name of	Continuing to teach all things
People from all nations.	The Father and of the Son and of the Holy Spirit.	That Jesus has commanded.

Lost ➡ **Correct Baptism** ➡ Saved

To be a disciple, it is not enough to simply be immersed in the waters; you must make this commitment to Jesus and his teachings. We must be eternal disciples because we never achieve complete knowledge. I became a disciple many years ago and I am a disciple today. My intention is to remain a disciple until the day I depart this physical world. While I am here, I am learning and practicing what I learn. This is my commitment. This is the commitment of every disciple.

Commitment to Jesus' truth is difficult. Jesus spoke of this commitment with these words.

> *If anyone would come after me, he must deny himself and take up his cross daily and follow me.*
> **Luke 9:23**

"If anyone would come after me...

he must deny himself

and take up his cross daily

and follow me

Luke 9:23

This is the commitment of every disciple. It is difficult and it is here compared to us taking up our cross. Our choice, our commitment is to Jesus in first place.

He is talking about the sacrifice required to be his disciple. The cross was an instrument of death used by the Romans at the time. Jesus is telling us that we must die to the old teachings we have received and follow him. We must kill our ego: "deny yourself." Our desire is to do what pleases us and sometimes what pleases the people around us. The influence of family, friends, colleagues, and society in general is extraordinarily strong. Our desire to please them must die.

Matthew recorded this teaching of Jesus like this.

> *Do not think that I came to bring peace on earth. I did not come to bring peace but a sword. For I have come to 'SET A MAN AGAINST HIS FATHER, A DAUGHTER AGAINST HER MOTHER, AND A DAUGHTER-IN-LAW AGAINST HER MOTHER-IN-LAW'; & 'A MAN'S ENEMIES WILL BE THOSE OF HIS OWN HOUSEHOLD.' He who loves father or mother more than Me is not worthy of Me. And he who loves son or daughter more than Me is not worthy of Me. And he who does not take his cross and follow Me is not worthy of Me. He who finds his life will lose it, and he who loses his life for My sake will find it.* **Matthew 10:34-39**

This teaching is difficult! Our choice, our commitment, is always to Jesus first. Anyone who is not ready to make this commitment should not be baptized. They are not ready to be saved, to be a disciple of Jesus.

For example, some of you who are reading this belong to churches that do not teach Jesus' will as written in the Bible when it comes to baptism and other teachings. These churches teach that people are saved without baptism. They teach that baptism comes after salvation. They teach things like "the sinner's prayer" as the moment of salvation, something the Bible does not even mention. They teach that baptism is "an outward sign of an inward change that has already taken place." It is a nice phrase, but it is not what the Bible says.

Those who are baptized are committed to Christ's truth about baptism and all his teachings and must reject the teachings to the contrary. These are teachings, which create the many divisions that we see in the religious world today.

Read what Paul said to those who made a commitment in Rome.

> Now I urge you, brethren, note those who cause divisions and offenses, contrary to the doctrine which you learned, and avoid them. For those who are such do not serve our Lord Jesus Christ, but their own belly, and by smooth words and flattering speech deceive the hearts of the simple. **Romans 16:17-18**

The right thing for someone in a church that does not teach the truth about baptism is to "note those"—that is, be careful and "avoid them." These are harsh words! We often have friends and family in these churches. We do not want to abandon them. Sometimes someone might say, "Oh, but I just want to stay with them so I can teach them the truth and get them out of these erroneous doctrines." The intentions are good! But in my experience, people fail to convert others this way, and they often end up corrupting themselves. Taking a firm stand and leaving at times says more to your family and friends than staying.

Paul says the following:

> *Do not be deceived: 'Evil company corrupts good habits.* **1 Corinthians 15:33**

If people can be won over, they can be won over to the truth by making a difficult decision to walk away from them (at least from their meetings) and teaching these truths to them on other occasions.

We have already seen that at the moment of our baptism; our sins are washed away (**Acts 22:16**). We also know that it is the blood of Christ that sets us free (**Revelation 1:5**). Blood sanctions biblical covenants. When Moses gave the first covenant (what we now call the "Old Covenant"), he sanctioned it with blood (**Hebrews 9:16-20**). Jesus said that his blood is the blood of the New Covenant (**Matthew 26:28**). The point is this: we have our sins washed away in baptism, and in baptism, the blood of Jesus sets us free. Through the blood of Jesus, at the moment of baptism, we enter into a covenant with Christ.

As we discussed at the beginning of this chapter, it is like the covenant or commitment of marriage. Paul uses marriage to illustrate the church's relationship with Christ. Or rather, he uses the relationship between Christ (the bridegroom) and his church (the bride) to illustrate how husbands should treat their wives. But here we learn about the church as well.

> *Husbands, love your wives, just as Christ loved the church and gave himself up for her, that he might sanctify her, cleansing her by the washing with water through the word.* **Ephesians 5:25-26**

The church is the bride of Christ, so Christ is the bridegroom. We have this covenant. But what does this have to do with baptism? Consider the idea in verse **26.**

> *Christ sanctified the church and purified the church by the washing with water through the word.*

Paul must be speaking of baptism here. Just as a bride must be pure and sanctified for her husband, so too must the church. We enter this covenant with Christ through this washing: baptism.

It is even simpler to say that we enter the church when we are saved: when we are baptized. On the day of Pentecost, **Acts 2:38,** Peter told his listeners what they should do:

> *Repent and be baptized every one of you in the name of Jesus Christ for the remission of sins, and you will receive the gift of the Holy Spirit.*

Immediately afterwards, Luke tells us:

> *Then those who accepted his message were baptized, and about three thousand were added to their number that day.* **Acts 2:41**

Faith in Jesus
Repentance of sins
Confession of Jesus as Lord

Baptism → Saved

We enter into a covenant with Jesus and we become a part of his bride, the church.

Notice the phrase "added to them that day" in some versions. To what were they added? In the King James Version Luke says:

> And the Lord added to the **church** daily those who were being saved. **Acts 2:47**

The word for church (ἐκκλησία) is not in some Greek texts. The texts used by the translators of the King James and New King James versions do include this word. Where else would they have been added? Many newer versions translate the phrase as added to "their number," "their fellowship," "the assembly," "the group," or similar. Most commentators recognize chapter two of Acts as the beginning of the church. What can we conclude? The saved are added to the church by the Lord.

In baptism, we receive the remission (forgiveness) of our sins and the gift of the Holy Spirit. At that very moment, the Lord adds us to His church. The church of Christ is the body of all the saved, washed, and sanctified people of the world.

We must be committed to this church of Christ. I am not speaking of the church of Christ as a denomination. I am speaking of the same church the apostles Peter, Paul, and John were part of. It is the church "the number," "the fellowship," "the assembly," or "the group," that is committed to the truth, and not only says so, but acts according to the standard set by Jesus. Paul said:

> but if I am delayed, I write so that you may know how you ought to conduct yourself in the house of God, which is the church of the living God, the pillar and ground of the truth. **1 Timothy 3:15**

We must distance ourselves from those who are not committed to the truth. We cannot be baptized if we do not make this commitment.

Baptism is the beginning, but those who are to be baptized must understand that the truth goes far beyond the truth about baptism. Many churches today have strayed in other ways as well. Sound biblical doctrine is a standard for the church to follow in all aspects. I found the expression "sound doctrine" or "sound words" in six different verses in three of Paul's letters: **1 Timothy 1:10; 1 Timothy 6:3; 2 Timothy 1:13; 2 Timothy 4:3; Titus 1:9; Titus 2:1.**

Look at what just these three of these say.

> Hold fast the pattern of sound words which you have heard from me, in faith and love which are in Christ Jesus. **2 Timothy 1:13**

For the time will come when they will not endure sound doctrine, but according to their own desires, because they have itching ears, they will heap up for themselves teachers. **2 Timothy 4:3**

If anyone teaches otherwise and does not consent to wholesome words, even the words of our Lord Jesus Christ, and to the doctrine which accords with godliness. **1 Timothy 6:3**

This sound doctrine becomes a "pattern," as Paul says in **2 Timothy 1:13**. In other versions this word pattern is replaced by the word "model."

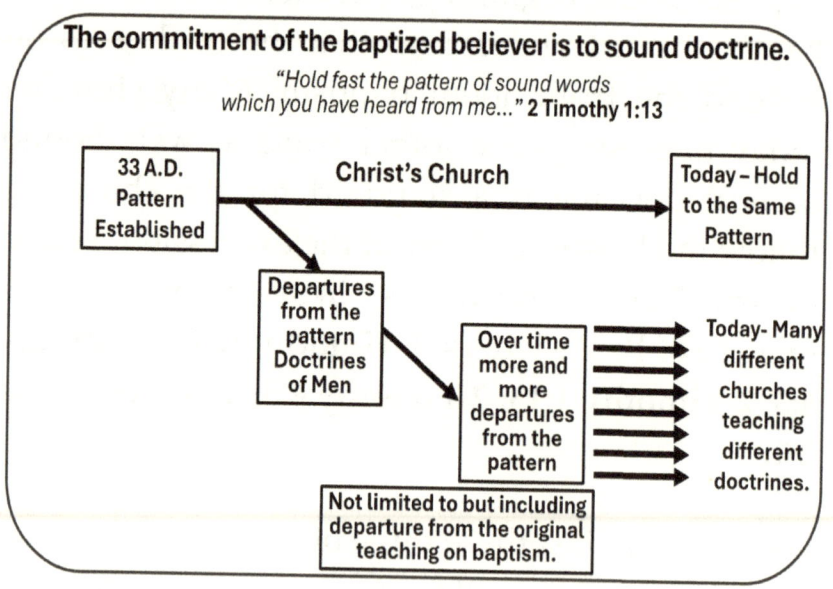

The commitment of the baptized believer is to sound doctrine.

"Hold fast the pattern of sound words which you have heard from me..." **2 Timothy 1:13**

33 A.D. Pattern Established

Christ's Church

Today – Hold to the Same Pattern

Departures from the pattern Doctrines of Men

Over time more and more departures from the pattern

Today- Many different churches teaching different doctrines.

Not limited to but including departure from the original teaching on baptism.

This means that the church has a standard to follow. The New Covenant gives us the model for our faith and practice. It is our standard for the plan of salvation, church worship, church organization, and the standard of morals and ethics in the daily lives of Christ's disciples. Those who are baptized should seek a congregation of Christ's church that also seeks to live this model.

Conclusion

Making the decision to be baptized is the most crucial decision anyone can make. By making this decision, your life will take a new direction that ends in Heaven with God. You are becoming a disciple of Jesus, following him and his truths. You have repented of your sins. Sin is everything that does not please God. Churches that practice human doctrines that do not follow the standard of sound doctrine revealed in Scripture do not please God, and we cannot be part of them, or we would be accomplices in their errors. This is the commitment the baptized person is making. The new convert's responsibility is to join a congregation of the church that belongs to Jesus, a church that follows the standard of sound doctrine revealed in the Bible.

"I want to be baptized, teacher, but there's no church like that near me. What should I do?" the question arises. Well, there are congregations of the church of Christ that follow sound doctrine throughout the world. However, this church still does not exist in some communities. We can either point you to the nearest church, or we can instruct you on how to start a congregation, which can even be done in your living room. We are together in

126

preaching the pure and simple gospel of Jesus Christ our Lord. If you are ready to make this commitment and enter into covenant with Christ and fellowship with your brothers and sisters, you are ready to be baptized. Contact us.

Additional Images

Pattern for Salvation
The Pure and Simple Gospel of Jesus

For I am not ashamed of the gospel of Christ, for it is the power of God to salvation for everyone who believes, for the Jew first and also for the Greek. **Romans 1:16**

Lost

Faith in Jesus
Repentance of sins
Confession of Jesus as Lord

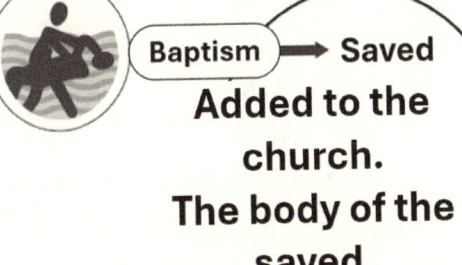

Added to the church.
The body of the saved.

Pattern of Worship

Let the word of Christ dwell in you richly in all wisdom, teaching and admonishing one another in psalms and hymns and spiritual songs, singing with grace in your hearts to the Lord. **Colossians 3:16**

Pattern established by Jesus through His apostles and prophets.

The Church the Jesus Built
- Praying to God in Edifying Assemblies
- Singing Praises to God Together
- Partaking of the Lord's Supper
- Giving to the Work of the Church
- Listening to the Word of God

Pattern of Governance
Organization

Simple and without a Hierarchy

But you, do not be called 'Rabbi'; for One is your Teacher, the Christ, and you are all brethren. **Matthew 23:8**

Pattern established by Jesus through His apostles and prophets.

Church of Jesus
Body of All the Saved

Every member acts according to their gifts.

Pattern of Ethics and Morality
Day to Day Lifestyle

We cannot live like this and still please God.
Now the works of the flesh are evident, which are: adultery, fornication, uncleanness, lewdness, idolatry, sorcery, hatred, contentions, jealousies, outbursts of wrath, selfish ambitions, dissensions, heresies, envy, murders, drunkenness, revelries, and the like... **Galatians 5:19-21**

Pattern established by Jesus through His apostles and prophets.

Galatians 5:22-23

Made in the USA
Columbia, SC
19 January 2026

77187644R00083